LAND AND LABOUR IN CHINA

LAND AND LABOUR
IN CHINA

by

R. H. TAWNEY

OCTAGON BOOKS

A DIVISION OF FARRAR, STRAUS AND GIROUX

New York   1972

Originally published 1932, by George Allen & Unwin Ltd. (London)

Reprinted 1964
by special arrangement with George Allen & Unwin Ltd.

Second Octagon printing 1972

OCTAGON BOOKS
A DIVISION OF FARRAR, STRAUS & GIROUX, INC.
19 Union Square West
New York, N. Y. 10003

For sale only in the United States of America
and dependencies

Printed in U.S.A. by
NOBLE OFFSET PRINTERS, INC.
NEW YORK 3, N. Y.

PREFATORY NOTE

The following pages, with the exception of the last chapter, were originally written as a memorandum for the Conference of the Institute of Pacific Relations held at Shanghai in November, 1931. They are concerned, not with the relations between China and the West, but with certain aspects of the economic life of China herself. Works on that subject are not very numerous, and I am informed that the memorandum contained matter which may be of interest to some English readers. It is accordingly reprinted here, with corrections and additions. The Institute has, of course, no responsibility for statements of fact or opinion contained in it.

It is obviously impossible for visitors to China, unacquainted with her language and unversed in her history, to make any original contribution to the study of her economic organisation and social problems. No more is attempted in the present work than to summarise some of the material contained in the more easily accessible publications, in the light of the information which those entitled to an opinion, both Chinese and foreigners, were good enough to supply to my wife and myself. At the risk of appearing pedantic, references have been given for the statements made, in order that the reader may see for himself the evidence on which they rest. Unfortunately three important books, Mr. Lionel Curtis's *The Capital Question of China*, Mr. Owen Lattimore's *Manchuria, Cradle of Conflict*, and Professor J. B. Condliffe's *China To-day: Economic*, appeared too late for us to make full use of them.

It is not possible for us to mention by name all those to whom our thanks are due. But we should like, in particular, to express our gratitude to the Institute of Pacific Relations and Dr. J. B. Condliffe, both for making possible our visit to China and for permission to reprint the results of it; the staff of the Agricultural College of the University of Nanking; Dr. Chang Po-ling, Professor Franklin Ho and Professor Fong, of the University of Nankai; Dr. L. K. Tao and his colleagues, of the Institute of Social Research; Dr. Y. C. James Yen and his fellow-workers of the Mass Education Movement at Ting Hsien; Dr. L. T. Chen, Dr. D. K. Lieu, and Professor J. B. Tayler. Mr. W. L. Holland helped us at every turn, and his assistance was most valuable. Our debt to Professor and Mrs. J. L. Buck, not only for being allowed to draw on their ample stores of knowledge, but still more for their counsel and inspiration, is too great to be acknowledged.

R. H. TAWNEY

CONTENTS

LAND AND LABOUR IN CHINA

CHAPTER I

INTRODUCTORY

China moved till yesterday in an orbit of her own, little
influencing the West and little influenced by it. Partly because
of her long isolation, partly because the foundations of her
own civilisation were singularly stable, partly as a result of
the new resources of science and technique to which the West
became heir in the nineteenth century, the perspective of her
recent history has been foreshortened. She had mastered
certain fundamental arts of life at a time when the West was
still ignorant of them. Like her peasants, who ploughed with
iron when Europe used wood, and continued to plough with
it when Europe used steel, she had carried one type of economic system and social organisation to a high level of achievement, and was not conscious of the need to improve or super-
sede it. For ages the most powerful agent in spreading civilisation in the East, it was not till less than a century ago that
she was forced against her will into continuous and intimate
contact with the civilisation of the West.

The phenomenon which disturbed the balance was the rise
of the great industry, first in England, and then, a generation
later, on the continent of Europe and in the United States.
The flood of economic change washed east and west. In
countries whose social institutions and intellectual traditions
had been adapted to the new order by a long process of development, it was harnessed, if with difficulty, without disaster. The
more different the conditions into which it penetrated from
those at its source, the more disturbing its results. In Europe,
where it started, it produced, side by side with a rapid increase
in income per head, a period of dislocation. In China, unprepared by her previous history to absorb and control them, the

new forces piled up against the dam, and the current, when
that broke, was the swifter and less manageable.

Their effect was aggravated by other elements of confusion,
which, in more favourable circumstances, they might have
helped to mitigate. One of the periods of anarchy, which are
a recurrent feature of Chinese history, was at its height within
a decade of the Treaty of Nanking. The appalling catastrophe
of the Taiping Rebellion, and the impotence of the Chinese
authorities to prevent or to end it, revealed a political system
crumbling from within at the moment when it was assailed
by growing pressure from without. When, thirty years later,
reform was attempted, under the shock of the *débâcle* of the
Japanese War, the event showed that the old régime could
neither resist change nor initiate it, so that everything in the
end gave way together.

As a consequence, economic, political and intellectual
movements, which elsewhere made their way by gradual
stages and small increments of growth, are, in the China of
to-day, in simultaneous ferment. The Renaissance; nationalism; the attempt to create a sovereign, unitary state, and its
struggle against local particularism and centrifugal ambitions;
the beginnings, on the eastern seaboard and rivers, of an
industrial revolution, with the criticisms and aspirations
which are its natural accompaniment; the reform of local
government, of education, of the financial system, and of the
complicated structure of Chinese jurisprudence; the partial
dissolution of the venerable institution of the Chinese family,
with the whole system of personal responsibilities and social
relations of which it was the centre—all these, and much else,
have been crowded into the space of little more than a generation. The forces, as always, interact; and a treatment which
dwells on one feature in the landscape to the neglect of the
remainder is necessarily artificial. It is even more misleading
to forget that the crucible in which the ferment takes place
is a mature civilisation, with a wealth of ripe experience and
fastidious canons of taste and conduct, which combines a
realistic respect for the practical achievements of the West

with a profound conviction of the ethical superiority of its own scheme of values.

The contrast of the present of China with its past is impressive. It is naturally the aspect of Chinese life which attracts the attention of the foreign observer. The West came to China, first as trader, secondly as missionary and educationalist, thirdly as financier and concessionnaire. By diplomacy and war, it succeeded in establishing its commercial outposts on small islands of privilege at the seaports and on the great rivers—outposts governed by oligarchies of western business men, and recalling, in their objects and methods, their relation to the Chinese, the political and economic advantages which they enjoyed and the criticisms which they provoked, the Steelyard of the Hanseatic League in London, or the factories of the Merchant Adventurers at Antwerp and Hamburg. It was inevitable, therefore, that the first contacts between China and the West should be those which had their origin in the commercial enterprise and ambitions of the latter. A modern fringe was stitched along the hem of the ancient garment. The furniture of western society, which stands a sea voyage better than its spirit, was unpacked at suitable points on the eastern seaboard. The economic frontier between the West and China was moved inland, so that the traveller who approaches the latter by way of Shanghai is tempted to reflect on the vanity of a pilgrimage which ends in a city so similar in externals to that in which it started.

Two generations later, the influence of the trader was reinforced by another, and more fundamental, movement. On the one hand, western educationalists were establishing schools and colleges in China. On the other hand, after an abortive experiment in the seventies, Chinese students began, at the end of the century, to visit in increasing numbers Japanese, American and European universities; by 1906, 12,000 were studying in Japan, and some 500 in the United States. Economic, political and military experience had shown to China the machine in action; now it saw for itself the conditions which generated the power that propelled it. In spite of the development of Chinese universities, the flow of students to foreign countries has continued, though on a somewhat smaller scale; in 1930, those granted permission by the Government to study abroad numbered 1,484, and the total number of Chinese students in foreign universities was in that year 5,032, of whom the majority were found in Japan and the United States.[1] It has been calculated that, of 566 persons eminent in Chinese public life, 27 per cent have received a university education in the United States, 16 per cent in Japan, and 14 per cent in different European countries.[2] Through the influence of such students, as well as through commerce, political contacts and war, China became increasingly aware of the results achieved by the application of science to the arts of production. Whatever their estimate of the more elusive qualities of the countries which they visited, the majority of them returned to their homes with the conviction that the secret of material progress was to be learned in the West.

The influence of western science, technology, economic conceptions, social theories and ethical standards on a civilisation which, half a century ago, if aware of them at all, regarded them with repugnance, is obviously a phenomenon of profound significance. Of the possibilities which it opens, and the problems caused by it, something is said below. But the embroidery must not be mistaken for the fabric, or the door for the house. "Yes, it is distressing; but it is not so bad as at the end of the Han dynasty, or, for that matter, of the T'ang, or indeed, when I come to think of it, as on the fall of the Mings"—men rarely in the West console themselves for public misfortunes by reflecting that they were worse under the Merovingians or during the Thirty Years' War, and the comment of a Chinese scholar on the present discontents of his country reveals the difference of perspective. China, as an organised community with a distinctive culture, was in the

[1] The highest registration of Chinese students in American universities and colleges was in 1924–25, when it reached the figure of 1,561.
[2] For detailed figures, see *Who's Who in China*, by H. O. Lanson, in *The China Critic*, November 20, 1930.

past the contemporary of Egypt and Mesopotamia. In spite of recurrent invasion, civil war and anarchy, her history spans, with impressive continuity, what in the West are regarded as separate epochs. The first duty of the visitor is to remember these truisms. It is to clear his mind of the optical delusion produced by Shanghai, which, to-day at least, is a gate into China, not China herself.

The country to which it leads is smaller in fact than it is in appearance, for great parts of it are sterile. It is thought to have an area of 1,897,000 square miles without its dependencies,[1] and of 4,282,000 with them. Its total population is uncertain,[2] but it is probably between a fifth and a sixth of that of the world, and the aggregate population of four out of its twenty-eight provinces exceeds that of France, Germany and Great Britain combined. The true analogy, applicable alike to the political and to the economic organisation of China, is not between China and a single European state, but between China and Europe as a whole. To travel from the seat of the National Government to Chengtu, the capital of the largest province, Szechwan, with an area of 220,000 square miles and a population of over fifty millions, may take longer than to go from the former to London. A hundred and fifty miles to the west of Chengtu can be seen, on a clear day, the peaks of the Chinese dependency of Tibet.

Long before the journey is completed, the wave of western economic life which beats in the East dies away into a ripple. Only the externals of social changes are statistically measureable, and a consideration of the progress of industrialisation is postponed till later. But this aspect of the problem of China is so fundamental and so generally discussed that it is desirable from the start to see it in perspective. The practice, not unknown even in reputable writers, of speaking of western civilisation as though it consisted of certain technical devices and economic methods introduced in the course of the last

---

[1] I.e. without Mongolia, Tibet and Sinkiang (Chinese Turkestan). The area of China exclusive of these (1,897,000 square miles) is about half that of the United States.   [2] See below, pp. 23–24.

century and a half would be too absurd for discussion, were its results not so mischievous. It is true, however, that among the more important of the material foundations on which that civilisation rests to-day are coal and iron, together with the railways and power-driven machinery which coal and iron make possible, and that the resulting technique may legitimately be compared with that of China.

In an area which is larger, if Russia be excluded, than that of Europe, there are at present some 9,500 miles of railway and approximately 35,000 miles of roads suitable for motor traffic; forty-one modern collieries, with an aggregate output amounting, when the small native mines are included, to about 25,000,000 tons; nine iron and steel companies, with a possible production of about 1,000,000 tons of pig iron and 110,000 tons of steel, and an actual production which, owing to political disturbances and economic depression, is less than half that amount. The industry in which factory production won in the West its earliest triumphs was that of cotton spinning, followed, at an interval, by other textiles. The cotton mills in China, according to the latest figures available, number 127, with approximately 4,000,000 spindles and 30,000 looms, and the steam silk filatures, 202; the number of woollen mills is uncertain, but, judged by the capital invested, is insignificant. In addition, there are about 500 electric light and power plants, between 190 and 200 flour mills, between 280 and 300 oil mills, about 190 match factories and, perhaps, 1,500 to 2,000 other establishments which may be described, to use the common, though ambiguous, expression, as modernised.[1]

Such figures, it is true, give an inadequate impression of the degree to which Chinese life has been affected by the advance of modern economic methods. The fact that the wares produced by the latter have penetrated, and that their competition is felt, in regions still unchanged in technique and

[1] For the progress of industrialisation, see Franklin L. Ho and H. D. Fong, *The Extent and Effects of Industrialisation in China*, 1929; H. D. Fong, *China's Industrialisation, A Statistical Survey*, 1931; L. K. Tao and S. H. Lin, *Industry and Labour in China*, 1931; and below, pp. 121–128 and Appendix.

economic organisation; the fact, again, that, precisely because they are massed at a few strategic points, large industrial concerns have a weight and power of attraction disproportionate to their number; the silent permeation of considerable ranges of Chinese society by the influence of western commerce, finance, education and science, are not reflected in them. The movement to industrialisation is a growing force. Where it directly affects, for better or worse, the livelihood of one, it indirectly modifies the habits of ten. Its effect on the mind, which is not susceptible of measurement, is ultimately more important than its visible embodiment in mills and mines.

Apart from these subtler reactions, industrialisation is less, rather than greater, in actual extent, than is suggested by statistics in which all undertakings are grouped together. Modern industry in China is limited to certain well-defined areas, is confined to certain branches of enterprise, and, to a considerable, though diminishing, degree, is under foreign management. Since there are, as yet, no through communications from north to south, or from east to west, the effect of railways is still local, rather than national, while modern roads exist mainly in the neighbourhood of large cities. Owing to the cost of transport, coal cannot easily be moved, in many parts of China, more than a few miles from the pit-head, and the great mass of the population must use other fuels. The consumption of iron and steel per head is approximately one hundredth that of England and one hundred-and-eightieth that of the United States, while over a quarter of the output of pig iron is produced by two firms. Of the 120 odd cotton mills, 58 are in Shanghai, and 25 in Wusih, two hours distant from it, 7 in Tientsin, and 6 in Hankow; of the total number of spindles and looms, approximately 40 per cent are owned by foreigners. The majority of the remaining undertakings of a modern type cling to the coastal region dominated by Shanghai, to the Yangtze basin, with its inland industrial centre of Wuhan, to the northern coalfields and Manchurian ports, and, to a less extent, to Canton and its hinterland. The multitude of currencies; the variety of weights and measures; the absence of adequate machinery for investment; the existence till recently of over seven hundred tax barriers levying duties on goods in transit; the small volume per head of foreign trade; the preponderance of raw materials and food-stuffs among Chinese exports; the fact that the source from which great fortunes are derived is still almost as often official perquisites and military plunder as the profits of industry; the paradoxical sentiment which esteems the sage more highly than the millionaire—such phenomena point to the same conclusion.

The hackneyed reference to the Middle Ages is sadly overworked, and leaves a good deal unsaid. It is misleading, indeed, both in principle and in detail. On the one hand, it implies a comparison of stages of development, as though the Chinese version of civilisation, instead of differing in kind from the European, were merely less mature. On the other hand, it ignores the sharp contrasts between them, not only—the most important point—in spirit and quality, but in circumstance and environment. The most obvious of the economic characteristics of mediaeval Europe—to mention no other—was that its population was small, its uncultivated area available for colonisation large, and its sea communications of exceptional excellence. The population of China is large, her unused land resources, except in Manchuria and the north-west, comparatively small, and the greater part of her territory, in spite of the rivers, difficult of access from the sea. It is true, however, that the technique and economic structure of seven-eighths of China recall, though with significant differences, the conditions which existed in Europe in the fifteenth century, outside the great commercial centres of Italy, Germany and the Low Countries, rather than those of its industrialised regions to-day.

In certain of the arts of production, and, still more, of life, she had been a pioneer. But the era of invention, which in the West followed that of natural science, in China preceded it. Having made her discoveries, she left it to peoples of coarser

fibre to reap their fruits, as though conscious that her own
genius required for its expression more sensitive media.
Methods once crystallised continued unchanged; for, these
methods being adequate, and often admirable, change was an
evil, which there were few prizes to induce, and no relentless
pressure of external circumstances to compel, her to undergo.
As far as the greater part of the country is concerned, the
plough, the loom, the manner of working in wood, metal and
clay, the relations of landlord and tenant, master and apprentice, creditor and debtor, the fundamental institutions of the
family, marriage and property, are held by good authorities
to have been altered but little during the period whose history
is known with certainty. What elsewhere is forgotten is in
China remembered; what elsewhere is a memory is in China a
fact. The forced labour which two thousand years ago built
the Great Wall out of countless humble lives is still recalled
with hatred by the common people. There are stretches of
the Grand Canal, still thronged with traffic, which were old
when Roman engineers were driving roads through Britain.
Save that they are armed with rifles, the bandits whose ex-
ploits fill the daily press are the bandits of Chinese novels
and plays of the age of Robin Hood.

Such contrasts between the static civilisation of China—as
it was formerly called—and the more mobile economy of the
West are easily drawn and easily misinterpreted. They are
misinterpreted when the differences which they emphasise are
assumed to be the expression of permanent characteristics.
History, with its record of the movement of leadership from
region to region, lends little support to the theory that certain
peoples are naturally qualified for success in the economic arts,
and others unfitted for it, even were the criteria of such success
less ambiguous than they are.

The traditionalism which has sometimes been described as a
special mark of Chinese economic life is the characteristic, not
of China, but of one phase of civilisation which Europe has
shared with her. Rapid economic change as a fact, and continuous economic progress as an ideal, are the notes, not of

the history of the West, but of little more than its last four centuries; and the European who is baffled by what appears to him the conservatism of China would be equally bewildered could he meet his own ancestors. During nearly a thousand years, the crafts of the husbandman, the weaver, the carpenter and the smith saw as little alteration in the West as they have seen in the East. In the former, as in the latter, common men looked to the good days of the past, not to the possibilities of the future, for a standard of conduct and criterion of the present; accepted the world, with plague, pestilence and famine, as heaven had made it; and were incurious as to the arts by which restless spirits would improve on nature, if not actually suspicious of them as smelling of complicity with malignant powers. In the former, as in the latter, political confusion, civil disturbance, brigandage and recurrent starvation were for generations the rule rather than the exception. It is true, however, that, for wide ranges of Chinese life, the contrast is valid, though the area to which it applies is year by year contracting. In technological equipment and industrial organisation, as in the foundations of law, psychology and social habits, on which both ultimately rest, the greater part of the West lives on one plane, the greater part of China on another.

What is true to-day is less true than yesterday, and may be false to-morrow. The forces which have caused the economic development of China and the West to flow in different channels are a fascinating theme for historical speculation, but they are one on which a layman is precluded from entering. Naturally, he will remind himself that the question is not merely why the economic life of China has not changed more, but why that of the West has changed so much. Naturally, certain commonplace considerations of geography, history, culture and social institutions will occur to his mind. Naturally, he will recall the position of China, with her vast and relatively homogeneous territory, isolated on the west by mountain barriers, and on the east in contact with civilisations inferior to her own, to whom she gave, and was conscious of giving, more than she received; her patriarchal family system which, far more than the state, has prevented the individual from being crushed by personal misfortune or social disorder, and has weakened the force of economic incentives by making his livelihood the concern and his earnings the property of the family group; the teeming population which that system encouraged and the obstacles to technical improvement offered by the cheapness of human labour; the influence of an educational policy devoted to the encouragement of academic culture and indifferent to the sciences by which man masters his environment; the philosophy of Chinese sages, with its scholastic contempt for the merchant and its idealisation of agriculture and the peasant; the small part played in the past by government and law, compared with personal relations, voluntary associations and local custom.

Naturally, he will compare these peculiarities with the characteristics of Europe. He will consider the significance of the long and deeply indented coastline of the latter, with its two inland seas in the south and north, which made foreign commerce possible for almost all her regions, and indispensable to some of them. He will recall her possession throughout history of numerous independent centres of economic energy, which fertilised each other by rivalry, imitation and actual migration, so that Italy, Spain and Portugal, France, Holland and England, not to mention, at a more recent date, Germany and the United States, became in turn her economic schoolmasters, and did for each other, though by different methods, what the West, as a whole, was to do later for China. He will ponder the impress stamped on her institutions by Roman law, and the ghost of past unity that, when anarchy was at its worst, still haunted her imagination. He will reflect on her early development of a powerful bourgeoisie based on trade and finance, which, first in Italy, then in Holland, and later in England, remade government, law and economic policy, and, when the scientific movement reborn at the Renaissance won its first great triumphs, was alert to turn them to practical account. He will remember the smallness, till recently, of the population of parts of the West in relation to its natural resources, and the consequent stimulus to technical invention.

These are problems, however, which an amateur, unversed in Chinese history and literature, cannot venture to discuss. He must leave the past development of China to the specialist, and confine himself to the task of attempting to note the salient facts in her present economic situation.

CHAPTER II

THE RURAL FRAMEWORK

The scientific study of Chinese society is still in its infancy. Such industrialism as exists, being novel, has been frequently described; but the massive and permanent background of the traditional economy has received less attention. In spite of admirable work by Chinese and foreign scholars, many aspects of the economic organisation and social structure of China are still but partially known. Nor, even were knowledge of the normal operations of her economic system more complete than it is, would it be easy to allow for the dislocation which it has undergone during a decade of disorder.

The population of China cannot be stated with certainty. Official censuses, usually of households, not persons, have been made for a longer period, and with greater regularity, than in any other country. They have been supplemented, since 1904, by the Maritime Customs estimates, and, since 1919, by the estimates made by the Postal Authorities. In addition, there are the data collected by private inquirers, and the deductions of statisticians from the materials assembled. The minimum estimate made by a public authority in the present century is 331,200,000, which was the figure given in 1910 by the Ministry of the Interior for China proper, without Tibet and Mongolia; the maximum is 485,600,000, which was that of the Post Office census for the same area in 1926. The latest Customs estimate is between the two; it gave a figure for 1929 of 438,900,000, exclusive of Shanghai, Nanking, Tientsin and Hankow.[1] It is improbable, perhaps, that the present popula-

---

[1] Figures from *The China Year Book*, 1929–30, pp. 1–4, and *Maritime Customs Report and Abstract of Statistics*, 1929, p. 250. For recent discussions, see papers before *XIXe Session de l'Institut International de Statistique*, 1930 (*An Estimate of the Population of China in 1929* by Warren H. Chen, *China's Population Problem* by Chang Heng Chen, *The Chinese Census of Population since 1712* by Chungshen S. Shen); *A Westerner's Effort to estimate the Population of China and its Increases* by W. F. Willcox; *A Study of China's Population Statistics* by C. M. Chen (*Statistical Monthly*,

tion of China is much less than 400,000,000, or much more than 450,000,000. But all the figures that are canvassed resemble the well-known estimate of the population of England made by Gregory King in 1696, in being based on inferences, not on ascertained facts. In the absence of the latter, detailed discussion is unprofitable.

The geographical distribution of this great population is extremely unequal. A large part of China, though much the smaller part of its total area, consists of a series of alluvial plains, lying between the mountains on the west and the sea on the east, and at certain points, along the great rivers, stretching far into the interior. Human beings are crowded in these plains and waterways. There is one great block, for example, in the basin of the Yellow River and on the northern plain, another in the lower Yangtze valley, a third on the Chengtu plain in Szechwan, and a fourth in the delta of Canton. The mean density of the population of China as a whole, exclusive of her dependencies, is not high. On the basis of the postal estimate for 1929, it is 254 per square mile, as compared with 192 in France, 352 in Germany, 483 in the United Kingdom and 680 in Belgium. But six-sevenths of her total population are thought to be massed in one-third of her territory, and the density is put at 614 in Shantung, 657 in Chekiang and 896 in Kiangsu.[1] In certain parts of these provinces, according to the investigations of the Famine Relief Commission, it is greater than that of either Japan or Bengal, reaching in some of them, it has even been stated, the astonishing figure of 6,000 per square mile, while in the plain of Chengtu, irrigated by an artificial system two thousand

Vol. II, No. 6, June, 1930); *Danger Spots in World Population* by Warren S. Thompson, pp. 30–32; articles in the *China Critic* of June 6 and 13, September 5, 12 and 26, 1930; *The Composition and Growth of Rural Population Groups in China* by C. H. Chiao and J. Lossing Buck (*Chinese Economic Journal*, Vol. II, No. 3, March, 1928).

[1] C. M. Chen, *op. cit.*, estimates that 17 provinces, accounting for 28 per cent of the area of China, contain 85·8 per cent of the population, with a mean density of 311 per square mile, and that 11 provinces, accounting for 15·6 per cent of the area, contain 63·7 per cent of the population, with a mean density of 414 per square mile.

years old, it is said to exceed 2,000.[1] What is striking in China is not the concentration in cities, great as some of these are, but the crowding of human beings on the land. To look over a plain from a low hill or city wall is to see a score of villages at once. They seem as thick on the ground as individual farms in western countries. In the words of an Italian traveller in the sixteenth century, who put the population of China at seventy millions, "of villages and hamlets (some of them containing a thousand households) the number is infinite; for the country is so covered with habitations, that all China seemeth but as one town."[2]

No complete occupational census of China has yet been taken. Certain features of her economy are known, and certain others are conjectured. The fundamental fact is the preponderance of the agricultural population. It is not open to question that the number of persons engaged in agriculture exceeds those employed in all other occupations together. Between 1914 and 1921 the Department of Agriculture and Commerce published statistics which, though defective, were sufficient to permit of some deductions being made from them. The conclusion of Dr. D. K. Lieu[3] and Dr. Chung Min-chen, of the Bureau of Economic Information, who have made a careful study of

---

[1] For figures, see J. B. Tayler, *The Study of Chinese Rural Economy* in the *Chinese Social and Political Science Review*, Vol. VIII, No. 1, January, 1924; *China, A Commercial and Industrial Handbook* (Washington, 1926), p. 11; W. H. Mallory, *China, Land of Famine* (New York, 1926). The figure of 6,000 per square mile is hardly credible, and it is probable that the data on which it was based were unreliable.

[2] Giovanni Botero, *Relationi Universali*, 1593, quoted by W. F. Willcox, *op. cit.*

[3] *Statistics of Farm Land in China* by D. K. Lieu and Chung Min-chen, in the *Chinese Economic Journal*, Vol. II, No. 3, March, 1928. A later inquiry was made in 1929 by the Bureau of Statistics of the Legislative Yuan. It obtained returns as to population from 1,229 *Hsien*, out of a total of 1,943, or 63 per cent, and as to cultivated land from 1,146 *Hsien*, or 59 per cent. The total households reported in the 1,229 *Hsien* were 56,697,071, of which 42,411,668, or 74·8 per cent, were farm households. If it be assumed that the *Hsien* not reporting contain households and farm households in the same proportion as those which did report, then the total number of households in China would be just under 90 million, and the total number of farm households about 67 million. The area of cultivated land reported by 1,146 *Hsien* was 796,795,157 mow. If it be assumed that *Hsien* not reporting had a proportionate area, then the total cultivated area would be about 1,350 million mow. (See M. T. Z. Tyau, *Two Years of Nationalist China* (1930), pp. 414–415.)

the data contained in them, is that in the year 1917–1918, the figures for which were least unreliable, the number of agricultural families amounted to 69,266,000 and the agricultural population to 345,780,000 persons, or 71 per cent of the population as estimated by the Post Office in 1926. There is no Black Country in China, and in only six of the provinces was the agricultural population less than 50 per cent of the total, while in ten it was over 60 per cent. Some good judges put the percentage for the country as a whole at a higher level than 71—at 75, 80, or even 85. No one, it appears, puts it at a lower.

The precise figure is less important, however, than the consensus of opinion that approximately three-quarters of the population are engaged in agriculture. China, though possessing important manufacturing industries, is preponderantly a nation of farmers, living in some hundred thousand villages or more, with perhaps ten times as many adjacent hamlets.[1] Her economic organisation, her culture, her past social traditions and present political problems, take their colour from that fact. A tolerable standard of well-being cannot be said to prevail as long as some considerable proportion of her rural population is under-fed and under-housed, decimated by preventable disease, and liable to be plunged in starvation by flood and drought. A stable state is equally difficult of creation until the social conditions of rural China have been substantially improved. Political organisation rests on economic foundations. When the latter crumble, it crumbles with them.

Agriculture is not a single industry, but a group of industries. The first striking feature of Chinese farming is one which it shares with the agriculture of Japan, but which distinguishes it sharply from that of Europe and America, and (though for different reasons) from that of India. It is the unimportance, except in the north-west, of animal husbandry. If, as some authorities have held, the Chinese were originally a people of the steppes, they had ceased to be pastoralists before history

[1] C. F. Remer, *The Foreign Trade of China* (Commercial Press, Shanghai, 1928), p. 235, quoting the report of the China Educational Commission, 1922.

begins. It is a question, not of climate or soil, but of resources and population. The relation between them has for many centuries been such that land capable of growing food for human consumption cannot be spared for raising beasts. Milk and meat will support fewer human beings than can be fed from the land which, if cattle were reared, would be required to grow fodder.

Hence not only is there, in China proper, no pasture farming, in the sense of an industry such as that of Denmark and large parts of England, specialising in the production of dairy produce and meat, but pasture as part of an arable rotation, as practised from time immemorial in most parts of the West, is virtually unknown. While in the principal European countries the percentage which it forms of the total cultivated areas is from 15 to 50, in China it is negligible. Wild grass, it is true, is highly valued and carefully preserved; the hills in the neighbourhood of villages in central China are in autumn shaved bare as with a razor. It is valued, however, not for grazing or winter fodder, but as fuel, partly consumed by the peasants themselves, partly carried into the nearest town and sold. It is sometimes suggested that land which, though unsuitable for tillage, might be used for grazing, is at present wasted, and that one way of improving the position of the peasants would be to persuade them to combine arable cultivation with animal husbandry. The idea is interesting, and it is possible that there are regions to which it is applicable. The truth appears to be, however, that, at any rate in central China, such land is already being employed for an indispensable purpose, which, under present conditions, cannot otherwise be served. In many parts of the country timber has been exhausted by the neglect or destruction of forests, while the cost of transporting coal more than a short distance is, in most regions, prohibitive. As a consequence, the provision of warmth is the business, not of the miner, but of the agriculturalist, so that grass is burned which in Europe or America would be fed to cattle or broken up by the plough.

Oxen are kept in the north and water-buffalo in the south,

but not for the sake of meat and milk, of which the former cannot be afforded, except at rare intervals, by the majority of villagers, and the latter is used only by foreigners. As in mediaeval Europe and in India to-day, they are primarily plough beasts; but they are fewer than in the latter, and probably than in the former, for there are no common pastures on which they can be grazed. There is an important export of wool from Tientsin, and the sheep kept are put at some 30,000,000. But, apart from the ubiquitous pig, which finds its own living, the Chinese consumer, except among the well-to-do, is almost a vegetarian, and the Chinese farmer not a dairyman, grazier or shepherd, but a cultivator.[1] The poor peasant of European tradition had a cow, but no land; the poor peasant in China has land, but no cow.

Much of China is uncultivable, owing to lack of moisture, excessive cold, mountains, or poverty of soil; but not all that is cultivable is actually cultivated. Estimates of the area under cultivation vary from a minimum of 180,000,000 to a maximum of 263,000,000 acres.[2] The materials used, however,

[1] The approximate number of livestock kept in China, as compared with those kept in India, is shown in the following table. That relating to China is taken from O. E. Baker, *Land Utilization in China*, in *Problems of the Pacific* (University of Chicago Press, 1928), p. 332, based on the statistical tables of agriculture and commerce, 1918 (Department of Agriculture and Commerce, Peking, 1922). That relating to India is taken from the Report of the Royal Commission on Agriculture in India, 1928, p. 168.

	China and Dependencies
Horses	4,702,200
Mules and Asses	5,239,782
Cattle	20,355,240
Swine	61,365,262
Sheep	28,500,617
Poultry	344,687,000

	British India	51 Indian States
Horses, Mules and Donkeys	3,200,000	1,000,000
Cattle and Buffaloes	151,000,000	36,000,000
Sheep and Goats	62,500,000	25,000,000
Camels	500,000	262,000

[2] Baker, *op. cit.*, p. 329, gives 180,000,000 acres. D. K. Lieu and Chung-min Chen, *Statistics of Farm Land in China* (*Chinese Economic Journal*, Vol. II, No. 3, March, 1928), p. 211, put the farm land of China at 1,687,000,000 mow, or approximately 253,050,000 acres. Other estimates, which I owe to the kindness of Professor J. L. Buck, are 263,000,000 acres (*Report of Agricultural Commission,*

are several years old, and, owing to the colonisation of Manchuria, the acreage has increased in the interval. China is a land of wide climatic differences, her territory extending in the south into the tropics and in the north to within 12 degrees of the Arctic Circle, while the rainfall varies from over 1,200 mm. in the extreme south to less than 450 mm. in the north of Manchuria, and the mean annual temperature from over 20 degrees centigrade in the former to under 5 degrees in the latter. When conditions are so diverse, the diversity of agriculture is naturally great, though, owing to bad means of communication, it is less than it might be, and less than it will be when railways and roads have increased, as in the West, the possibility of local specialisation. There are certain well-defined surplus and deficiency areas; but the situation of large parts of China, including some of the most densely populated districts, is what that of many regions in Europe was before the nineteenth century. Owing to the impossibility of moving food in bulk, they must either feed themselves or starve.

Geographers have distinguished six, ten and fourteen regions in China, but the fundamental agricultural division is the conventional one, which is cultural and political, as well as economic. It is between the south and the north, the dividing line running between the Yangtze and the Yellow River. The former is predominantly a land of high rainfall—in the Yangtze valley between 1,000 and 1,500 mm.—multiple crops and water-farming, carried on in valleys or on terraced hill-sides. In addition to rice, its characteristic crop and foodstuff, its typical products are silk, sugar and tea. The latter is a country of lower and more irregular rainfall, severe winters, recurrent drought, and dry farming, with wheat, millet, kaoliang, beans and maize as its staple crops. Overlapping the two, and stretching north from the Yangtze to the Hwai River, a distance of some 150 miles, is an intermediate region,

1914), and 246,000,000 (*Sixth Report on Crops and Markets*, May 31, 1923). There is reason to think that Professor Baker underestimates the area cultivated and overestimates that capable of cultivation.

where the agricultural features of south and north fade into each other. The following figures, compiled by Professor Baker from the statistics published by the Department of Agriculture and Commerce for 1914–18, give an estimate of the acreage under five crops, accounting together for 77 per cent of the total cultivated area, on the assumption that the latter is 180,000,000 acres:[1]

Crop	Acreage	Per Cent of Total Cultivated Area
Rice (average 1916–18)	50,000,000	27·9
Wheat (average 1914–18)	50,700,000	28·2
Corn (average 1914–17) ..	8,000,000	4·4
Barley (average 1914–18)	10,730,000	5·9
Grain Sorghums (2- and 4-year averages)	19,000,000	11·1

The contrast between the farming of the north-east, north and south, may be illustrated by later figures, which embody some of the results of the agricultural census now in process of compilation:

FARMS, LAND AND CROPS IN SIX PROVINCES

(*Areas in Acres*)

	Kirin and Liaoning	Hopei and Shansi	Kiangsu and Chekiang
Total farm households ..	2,716,000	6,098,000	8,222,000
Farm households as percentage of all households	78·5	84·0	74·0
Total acreage of principal crops	20,754,150	28,282,200	30,212,850
Average acreage per farm household	8·76	4·20	2·33
Percentage of irrigated land..	2	7	49*
Percentage of non-irrigated level land	75	71	45
Percentage of non-irrigated hilly land	23	22	6

* Approximate percentage. The percentage of irrigated land is 38·7 per cent for Kiangsu and 72·5 per cent for Chekiang.

It will be seen that in Kirin and Liaoning 2 per cent of the land is irrigated, and in Hopei and Shansi 7 per cent, com-

[1] Baker, *op. cit.*, p. 337. It must be remembered, here and elsewhere, that there is double cropping on much of the land.

pared with about 49 per cent in Kiangsu and Chekiang, and
72 per cent in Chekiang alone. The following table shows
that in the first group, 55·7 per cent of the total crop area
is under soy beans and kaoliang; in the second 48 per cent is
under wheat and millet; in the third 29·6 per cent is under
rice and 25·4 per cent under wheat. In Chekiang the acreage
under rice is 67 per cent of the total crop area.

ACREAGE OF PRINCIPAL CROPS IN SIX PROVINCES
(In Acres, and also as a Percentage of the Total Crop Area in Each Region)

Crop	Kirin and Liaoning		Hopei and Shansi		Kiangsu and Chekiang	
	Acres	Per cent	Acres	Per cent	Acres	Per cent
Millet	3,959,900	16·7	6,413,800	22·7	325,000	1·1
Kaoliang ..	5,718,450	27·5	4,720,950	16·7	1,030,050	3·4
Corn	1,930,800	9·3	2,935,050	10·3	754,650	2·5
Wheat ..	2,021,550	9·7	7,176,900	25·3	7,669,950	25·4
Barley ..	464,250	2·2	927,300	3·3	4,016,400	13·3
Rice	429,300	2·1	100,950	—	7,409,350	24·5
Glutinous rice..	195,900	—	34,050	—	1,533,600	5·1
Soy beans ..	5,848,800	28·2	1,957,800	6·9	3,337,800	10·6
Small beans ..	141,900	—	—	—	282,600	—
Broad beans ..	1,800	—	6,600	—	402,750	1·3
Black beans ..	—	—	453,900	1·6	—	—
Cotton	149,100*	—	1,469,250	5·2	1,916,700	6·4
Peanuts ..	123,600*	—	424,950	1·5	335,250‡	—
Irish potatoes ..	43,050§	—	197,550†	—	6,900¶	—
Sweet potatoes..	53,850*	—	228,100	—	661,950	2·2
Rape	—	—	31,200†	—	326,400	1·1
Sesamum ..	6,150	—	45,600‖	—	—	—
Tobacco ..	16,500	—	2,150†	—	49,500¶	—
Peas	—	—	85,200	—	93,150	—
Tsitz	50,850	—	239,850	—	—	—
Broon corn ..	43,200	—	—	—	—	—
Oats	—	—	546,150†	—	—	—
Sugar cane ..	—	—	—	—	21,300¶	—

* Liaoning only.   † Shansi only.   ‡ Kiangsu only.
§ Kirin only.   ‖ Hopei only.   ¶ Chekiang only.

Agriculture in China is a peasant industry. It is the business
of some seventy million farmers and their families. Small-scale
cultivation may co-exist with a régime of great landed estates,
as in the France of the eighteenth century and the Ireland of
the nineteenth. But there is no landed aristocracy in China;

when great estates are formed, they normally disappear in a few generations by division among heirs; and, while in parts of the country small absentee landlords are numerous, large landlords, though they exist in certain regions, are few. The area of cultivated land which is publicly owned, compared with that in the hands of private individuals, is also small. The policy pursued during the earlier part of the Tsing dynasty when, owing to civil war and confiscation, large tracts of land were at the disposal of the Government, was to bring them into cultivation by granting them free, or on easy terms, to such persons as would work them, and the area of public land thus made productive is stated to have amounted by 1887 to some thirty million acres.[1] Considerable areas are at present owned by the state, by quasi-corporate bodies such as clans, villages, temples, monasteries and educational institutions, and by private individuals.[2] Such lands, however, are normally leased in small parcels. Though official statistics have been published grouping holdings by their sizes, no information is available as to the total acreage contained in each group, and it is impossible to state, therefore, what proportion of land is let in large farms. But neither the direct cultivation of a great estate by its owner, on the Prussian model, nor, except here and there, large leasehold farms of the English type, obtain in China, and crops which elsewhere are grown by wage-labour

---

[1] Shao-Kwan Chen, *The System of Taxation in China in the Tsing Dynasty, 1644–1911* (Columbia University Press, 1914), p. 49. See also Han Liang Huang, *The Land Tax in China* (Columbia University Press, 1918), pp. 57–73, and Yuen Ming Pao, *Des Systèmes agraires en Chine* (Université de Changhai, 1922).

[2] Figures of the public land (classified as ancestors' land, village land and school land) in the province of Kwangtung are given in T. C. Chang, *The Farmers' Movement in Kwangtung* (National Christian Council of China, 1928), pp. 39–41. They are stated there to amount to one third of the total area of the province. See also Chi Yu Tang, *An Economic Study of Chinese Agriculture* (1924), pp. 234–236, where an example is given of clan land amounting in five villages to 860 acres. Statistics kindly supplied to me by Dr. Fong, and based on the returns of the Department of Agriculture and Commerce, 1912–20, show that (1) the National Government then owned forest land in ten provinces and administrative districts: in five of them it owned over 40 per cent of the total area, in the remainder its ownership was negligible; (2) that local governments owned forest land in all provinces and administrative districts, and in eleven of them more than 15 per cent of the total area.

on plantations, such as tea and cotton, are in China cultivated by peasant farmers. Whatever the scale of ownership, the rule in China, as in Japan and India, is *la petite culture*.

No comprehensive figures are available of the total number of agricultural wage-workers, as distinct from the farmers and the members of their families. While conditions vary widely, no doubt, from district to district, such local investigations as have been made suggest that they form only a small minority of the rural population; a study made of 5,255 families in the neighbourhood of Ting Hsien,[1] for example, showed that, of 10,803 males over 13 years of age, 9,011, or 83 per cent, were farmers, and 139, or 1·3 per cent, farm hands. Further light is thrown on the subject by the valuable researches of Professor Buck. Their result is to show that, on 2,866 farms in 17 localities in east, central and north China, the number of labourers hired by the year was 663, or one to every 4⅓ farms. The use of hired labour varied with the size of the farms, with the crops grown, and, of course, as far as labourers engaged by the day were concerned, with the season. Labour hired yearly and by the day formed 19·5 per cent of the total labour cost on the farms, but varied from 4·3 per cent on small farms to 14·3 per cent on those of medium size, and 31·6 per cent on large farms. In all, just over two-fifths of the farm labour was performed by members of the farmers' families, just under two-fifths by the farmers themselves, and just under one-fifth by hired labour.[2] The same conclusion is suggested by the small proportion of families in Chinese villages who are found, on inquiry, to be neither land-owners nor tenants, and for whom, therefore, wage-labour is the only alternative.[3] As in all coun-

---

[1] These figures, which I owe to the kindness of the Survey Department of the Mass Education Movement at Ting Hsien, are provisional and subject to correction. The occupations of the 10,803 males over 13 years were returned as follows:

Farmers ..	.. 9,011	Skilled labour ..	206	Military ..	.. 168
Farm hands	.. 139	Unskilled labour	137	Government service	47
Commercial	.. 424	Educational ..	185	Others ..	.. 486

[2] Buck, *Chinese Farm Economy* (Commercial Press, Shanghai, 1930), pp. 231–237.
[3] See, e.g., J. B. Tayler, *Farm and Factory in China* (1928), p. 106, where it is shown that out of 3,532 families only 592, or 16 per cent, were without land.

tries where the unit of agriculture is the family farm, the number of employees is substantially less than the number of employers. The agricultural wage-workers of China, like those of France, south Germany and Denmark, do not form a distinct class, differing sharply in economic position from the farmers for whom they work, but are scattered up and down the interstices of a society based on a multitude of little properties. Whatever her rural problems may be, they are not complicated by the existence of a landless proletariat. The typical figure in Chinese country life is not the hired labourer, but the land-holding peasant.

The conditions of his tenure vary widely from region to region, and even from village to village. According to the figures published by the Department of Agriculture and Commerce for 1918, about 50 per cent of the peasants were occupying owners, 30 per cent were tenants and 20 per cent owned part of their farm land while renting the remainder.[1] A later inquiry,[2] based on a sample investigation, gives a result which is substantially the same; the owners, it was found, formed 51·7 per cent, the tenants 22·6 per cent and the part-owners 22·1 per cent.

The differences in the proportions of the three classes in different provinces were, in each case, striking. The proportion of owners was highest in the northern provinces, somewhat less in the north-eastern, less still in the central, and least in the southern. In Shensi, Shansi, Hopei, Shantung and Honan, the first inquiry put it at 65 and the second at 69 per cent. In Kiangsi, Hunan and Kwangtung it was 31·8 per cent in the

[1] The figures are reproduced by Chi Yu Tang, *An Economic Study of Chinese Agriculture*, pp. 241–242, from which I have taken them. There appears to be no historical study of land tenure in China in a European language. Some, though fragmentary, information on conditions towards the end of the last century is contained in *Tenure of Land in China and the Conditions of the Rural Population*, in the *Journal of the China Branch of the Royal Asiatic Society*, New Series, Vol. XXIII, 1888, pp. 59–183. See also Yuen Ming Pao, *Des Systèmes agraires en Chine*, 1922.

[2] C. C. Chang, *A Statistical Study of Farm Tenancy in China* (*China Critic*, September 25, 1930).

first and 27 in the second. More limited investigations show similar contrasts.[1]

Such figures, even if reliable, leave a good deal unsaid. As all acquainted with the history of land tenure are aware, ownership and tenancy are somewhat treacherous terms. Their legal is not always identical with their economic connotation, and there are many types of agrarian system to which, unless carefully qualified, they are not applicable. In China, as in mediaeval Europe, the state has been weak, and local particularism strong. Custom, which means in effect the law of the locality, has created rights as secure, and obligations as binding, as those which in the West have been established by legislation.

[1] Figures for 75 villages in north-west Chekiang, which I owe to the kindness of Dr. L. K. Tao and his colleagues of the Institute of Social Research, Peiping, show that 32·9 per cent of the farmers were owners, 36·7 tenants and 30·4 tenants and part-owners. The Survey Department of the Mass Education Movement at Ting Hsien was so good as to supply me with the following provisional figures relating to 790 farms in 6 villages in Hopei:

Tenure	Per Cent of Total	Number of Mow Cultivated	Average Cultivated Land per Farmer, Mow
Owners	70·8	14,662	26·2
Part Owners	27·8	5,563	25·3
Tenants	1·4	141	12·8
Total (790)	100·0	20,366	25·8

The tenure of land held by 1,800 families was as follows:

Tenure	Per Cent of Total Families	Per Cent of Total Area
Owners	47·9	45·5
Part Owners	28·4	23·3
Tenants	10·0	7·8
Landlords	8·6	23·4
Labourers	1·4	0·0
Neither landlords nor farmers ..	3·7	0·0

Buck, *op. cit.*, pp. 145 *et seq.*, gives figures for 2,866 farms, which show that in the north China villages investigated by him, owners, tenants and part-owners formed respectively 76·5 per cent, 10·1 per cent and 13·4 per cent of the total, and in the east China villages 63·2 per cent, 17·1 per cent and 19·7 per cent. Tayler (*The Chinese Social and Political Science Review*, Vol. VII, No. 2, April, 1924) gives 89·3 per cent as the proportion of land cultivated by owners in certain villages in Chihli, and 36·6 per cent as the corresponding figure for certain villages in Kiangsu.

Unless, therefore, the custom of a region is known, a mere classification of peasants into owners and tenants may on occasion conceal as much as it reveals. In Chekiang, for example, it is stated, the rule is that the tenant owns the surface and the landlord the subsoil. The former has a right to renewal, cannot be evicted while he pays his rent, and can sub-let; the tenant right is freely mortgaged, sold and transmitted by inheritance; the cost of permanent improvements is divided between tenant and landlord. In the neighbourhood of Wuhu, where a similar custom obtains, the value of the landlord's interest was put in 1926 at $30[1] per mow and of the tenant's at $50 per mow. In Kwangtung tenants are stated to have a right to renewal provided that they have fulfilled the conditions of the lease. In the district of Changshu, in Kiangsu, where most of the land is owned by absentee landlords, the tenant-right is said to be equally well established. Where the conditions are those described as prevailing in Chekiang, custom has created what is, in effect, a system of dual ownership, and the position of the tenant recalls that of the Indian "right-holder," of the copy-holder of inheritance of past English history, or of the French *censier* under the old régime, though without the burdens that rested on the last. But cases in which the custom is unfavourable to the tenant appear to be equally, if not more, common. Nor must it be forgotten that the nominal owner is often little more than the tenant of a money-lender.

The real facts of the situation cannot be ascertained without further investigation than has yet been undertaken; but, in view of such evidence as is available, the statement that land tenure is not a problem in China, is, it may be suggested, unduly optimistic. Apart from the question of tenant-right, the relations between landlord and tenant are of extreme diversity. Agreements may be verbal or in writing. They may run from three to twenty years or more; or the tenant may hold merely at will, and be subject to eviction at the landlord's discretion. Rent may be paid in cash, in produce, or in both.

[1] Here and elsewhere, unless otherwise stated, dollars are Mexican dollars.

The landlord may be responsible for the equipment of the holding and for the provision of part of the working capital, or he may be merely parasitic, spending nothing on the land, and employing an agent to screw rack-rents out of tenants whose names are unknown to him. In parts of the country a common form of tenure is some type of *métayage*, under which the risks are shared between landlord and tenant, the former supplying part of the seed and sometimes, in addition, a wind-mill, irrigation pump and some of the farm cattle, the latter paying him one-fifth, one-half, or even three-fifths of the produce.

If ownership be interpreted in the strictest sense, it is possible that the estimate that approximately one-half of the peasants in China own their farms is not far from the truth. In that case, the proportion which peasant proprietors form of the total farming population is not noticeably high. It is larger than in Japan, Germany and the United States, but less than in France, Denmark and Ireland. The distribution of different forms of tenure is influenced by the past history, soil conditions, types of farming and general economic environment of different parts of China. Occupying ownership is least prevalent in the proximity of great cities where urban capital flows into agriculture—in the Canton delta 85 per cent of the farmers, and in the neighbourhood of Shanghai 95 per cent, are said to be tenants—and most general in the regions but little affected by modern economic developments. The provinces of Shensi, Shansi, Hopei, Shantung and Honan, where some two-thirds of the farmers are stated to be owners,[1] are the original home of Chinese agriculture. They have been little touched as yet by commerce and industry. The yield of the soil is too low to make it an attractive investment to the capitalist, while the farmer has not the resources to rent additional land. In the south, where the soil is more productive, agriculture yields a surplus; the commercialisation of economic relations has proceeded further; and both the induce-

---

[1] If those who are partly owners, partly tenants, be included among the owners, the proportion of owners is increased to between two-thirds and three-quarters.

ment and the ability to invest capital in land are accordingly greater. It is reasonable to expect that, with the expansion of modern industrial and financial methods into regions as yet unaffected by them, similar conditions will tend to establish themselves in other parts of the country. In that case, the struggle which has so often taken place in Europe between the customary rights of the peasant, farming largely for subsistence, and the interest of the absentee owner in making the most of his speculation is likely, it may be anticipated, to be repeated in China. In parts of the country, it is being repeated already.

The system of cultivation obtaining in China is marked by characteristics which, though they have their parallels in other eastern countries, are strikingly different from those associated with the agriculture of Europe, and, still more, of America. The first is familiar, for it strikes the eye of the most casual observer. It is the minuteness of the parcels into which land is divided.[1] The tiny patches separated by balks, which diversify the vast and solemn landscape of great parts of China, give the impression of an agriculture of pygmies in a land of giants.

This appearance is the result of two separate phenomena, which are due to different causes and which present different problems. The first may be called the sub-division of holdings:

[1] The following provisional figures kindly supplied by the Survey Department of the Mass Education Movement, Ting Hsien, illustrate the smallness of the fields in certain districts. They give the size of those worked by 200 families.

Size of Fields		Number of Fields	Per Cent
Under 1 mow		49	3·1
1–1·9	,,	233	15·0
2–2·9	,,	329	21·2
3–3·9	,,	250	16·2
4–4·9	,,	209	13·5
5–9	,,	370	23·8
10–14	,,	64	4·1
15–19	,,	21	1·4
20–24	,,	16	1·0
25–29	,,	6	0·4
30–34	,,	3	0·2
35–39	,,	1	0·06
40–	,,	1	0·06
Total	..	1,552	

it is the fact that the acreage in the tenure of a single family is usually small, and sometimes insignificant. The second may be called the fragmentation of cultivation: it is the fact that, whatever the size of the holding, the pieces composing it are physically dispersed. As in Europe, before the agricultural reconstruction of the last two centuries, in the unenclosed parts of it to-day, and in modern India and Japan, a Chinese farm does not normally lie in a compact block. It consists of anything from five to forty scattered squares, oblongs, strips, wedges and corners of land, scattered over hedgeless fields, and sometimes at a distance of more than a mile from each other.[1] The reasons given for this arrangement by peasants in China are the same as those given in the past by peasants in Europe. Land varies in quality from acre to acre; one man must not have all the best land, and another all the worst; a farmer needs both dry and wet land, hilly land for fuel and manure as well as level land for his crops; the dispersion of plots enables him to pool his risks of flood and drought. Once the arrangement is established, it is perpetuated and extended by the effect of inheritance. The rule hitherto having been equal partition, the grounds which caused fragmentation to be accepted as natural in the first place have caused each heir to receive part of each of the different kinds of land of which a farm is composed.

The varying methods by which, in different European countries, the scattered strips of the open-field village were formed into compact holdings are a matter of history. In Japan consolidation has been undertaken at the initiative of the Government and under its supervision. In India it has

---

[1] This feature is illustrated by the following figures of non-contiguous plots per farm on 78 farms in Shentze Hsien, Hopei, which I owe to Dr. L. K. Tao and his colleagues of the Institute of Social Research.

No. of Plots per Farm	Size of Plots (in Mow)			Distance (in Li) of Plots from the Farmstead		
	Average	Minimum	Maximum	Average	Minimum	Maximum
6·1	4·7	·2	34·0	1·78	Closely adjacent	6·0

1 Local Li = 0·58 Kilometre.

been encouraged by legislation and administrative action, and was the subject of recommendations by the last Commission.[1] In China itself legislation on the subject was passed in 1930.[2] Even when allowance is made, however, for the impression produced on the observer by local dispersion, the pattern of Chinese agriculture still remains minute. The more serious problem is the smallness of the acreage in the tenure of individuals.

The only comprehensive figures of the size of farm holdings in China were those collected more than ten years ago by the Department of Agriculture and Commerce.[3] They showed, if correct, that, out of the total of 49,359,591 farms represented in them, 36 per cent were below 10 mow (1·5 acres)[4], 26 per cent from 10 to 29 mow (1·5 to 4·3 acres), 25 per cent from 30 to 49 mow (4·5 to 7·3 acres), 10 per cent from 50 to 99 mow (7·5 to 14·85 acres), and 6 per cent of 100 mow (15 acres) and over. The average holding for the country as a whole was 24 mow, or 3·6 acres,[5] but it varied widely from one part of China to another. In the two north-eastern provinces of Heilungkiang and Kirin it was 127·5 mow (19·1 acres) and 110·5 mow (16·6 acres) respectively. In Shensi, Shansi, Hopei, Shantung and Honan it was 23·6, 35·5, 19·3, 20·7 and 56·1 mow (3·5, 5·3, 2·9, 3·1 and 8·4 acres). In Chekiang, Szechwan, Yunnan and Kweichow it was 8·2, 9·2, 8·0, and 7·0 mow (1·2, 1·4, 1·2 and 1·0 acres). The figures may be compared with those for Japan and India. In the former, 74 per cent of the holdings were stated in 1923 to be under 10 tan (2·4 acres). In the latter, the number of cultivated acres per cultivator was given by the census of 1921 as 12·2

---

[1] Report of the Royal Commission on Agriculture in India, 1928, Chapter 5.

[2] Land Law, Section 1, Chapter 3, Arts. 18–20 (*Ministry of Communications Gazette*, July 12, 1930). See below, p. 84.

[3] The figures for 1917 are reproduced by Chi Yu Tang, *An Economic Study of Chinese Agriculture* (1924), p. 251, from whom I take them.

[4] The size of the mow varies in different parts of China. The standard adopted by the Peiping Government in 1915 was 6·59 mow to one acre. This standard is followed in the calculations made in the text.

[5] *Statistics of Farm Land in China*, by D. K. Lieu and Chung Min-chen, Table 5 (*Chinese Economic Journal*, Vol. II, No. 3, March, 1928), who use, however, different figures from those given by Chi Yu Tang.

in Bombay, 9·2 in the Punjab, 4·9 in Madras, 3·1 in Bengal, 3·0 in Assam and 2·5 in the United Provinces.[1]

The return made with regard to the size of holdings in China possessed various defects,[2] and not much confidence can be placed in it. More reliable investigations into limited areas yield, however, much the same results.[3] They give a picture

[1] For Japan, see *Land Utilisation in Japan*, by Dr. S. Nasu, 1929; and for India the Report of the Royal Commission on Agriculture in India, 1928, p. 133.

[2] Apart from the fact that four provinces were omitted from it, it is not clear by what method, if any, the differences in the size of the mow in different districts (see above, p. 40, note 4) have been reduced to a common standard. The figures published by the Department of Agriculture and Commerce appear, nevertheless, to be the basis on which nearly all the generalisations as to the size and distribution of holdings in China are based.

[3] The evidence is necessarily fragmentary, but, as the question of the size of farms is important, it is perhaps worth while to summarise part of it. The Survey Department of the Mass Education Movement, Ting Hsien (Hopei), has been good enough to let me see the provisional results of an investigation in process of being carried out. The figures as to the size of farms relate to 790 farms in 6 villages. They are as follows:

Number of Mow Cultivated	Owners	Part Owners	Tenants	Total	Per Cent
0– 4·9	70	3	1	74	9·4
5– 9·9	112	24	4	140	17·7
10–14·9	73	47	3	123	15·6
15–19·9	66	36	1	103	13·0
20–24·9	44	22	0	66	8·3
25–29·9	36	21	1	58	7·3
30–34·9	32	25	0	57	7·2
35–39·9	13	9	0	22	2·8
40–44·9	17	7	1	25	3·2
45–49·9	14	3	0	17	2·2
50–54·9	16	4	0	20	2·5
55–59·9	13	2	0	15	1·9
60–64·9	10	6	0	16	2·0
65–69·9	5	3	0	8	1·0
70–74·9	8	4	0	12	1·5
75–	30	4	0	34	4·4
Total ..	559	220	11	790	100

The size of 10,290 farms in 62 villages was as follows:

Farms			Number	Per Cent
Large (over 100 mow)	..	..	220	2·1
Medium (50–100 mow)	..	..	1,228	12
Small (0–50 mow) ..	..	..	8,842	85·9
Total	..	..	10,290	100·0

[*Footnote continued on page 42*

of an agricultural system based on a multitude of tiny holdings, the largest being found in the north-east, where land is still abundant, the next largest in the northern provinces of China proper, and the smallest in the south, where climate, soil, irrigation, and the double cropping facilitated by them, make it possible for a morsel of land to yield a living. Nor do statistics of the size of holdings tell the whole story. The normal unit of Chinese rural society is the patriarchal family, composed of three or more generations living together, and augmented by

The number of mow cultivated in these 62 villages was as follows:

Farms			Number of Mow	Per Cent of Total
Large (over 100 mow)	..	..	32,800	13·7
Medium (50–100 mow)	..	..	73,657	30·9
Small (0–50 mow) ..	..	..	132,099	55·4
Total	..	..	..	238,556	100·0

I am indebted to Dr. L. K. Tao and his colleagues of the Institute of Social Research, Peiping, for the following figures of the size of farms in 68 villages in the north-western part of Chekiang province:

Size of Farm					Percentage of Farmers
Under 5 mow	..	..	..	..	38·0
6–10 ,,	..	..	..	..	33·0
11–25 ,,	..	..	..	..	20·6
26–50 ,,	..	..	..	..	6·6
51–100 ,,	..	..	..	..	1·6
101–200 ,,	..	..	..	..	0·2
Over 200 ,,	..	..	..	..	0·0
Total	..	..	..	..	100·0

Both the preponderance of small farms and the larger proportion of very small farms in Chekiang are noticeable. For other evidence, see Buck, *Chinese Farm Economy*, p. 46, who gives the median of 2,866 farms investigated as 2·13 hectares (5·1 acres); Tayler, *Farm and Factory in China*, p. 106, who shows that, out of 2,940 families with land, 32·9 per cent had less than one acre; *The Chinese Economic Bulletin*, Vol. XV, No. 33 (December 7, 1929) for figures showing that in Changsha (Kiangsu) 8 per cent of the farms were under 5 mow (0·75 acre), 54 per cent 5–15 mow (0·75 to 2·25 acres), 33 per cent 15–50 mow (2·25 to 7·5 acres) and 5 per cent over 50 mow (7·5 acres); *Chinese Economic Monthly*, Vol. II, No. 10 (October, 1926), giving particulars of four villages in Suiyuan, in which the percentages of holdings under 8 acres were 95, 89, 65 and 96; *ibid.*, Vol. V, No. 3 (September, 1929), giving the average of 543 farms in six provinces as 1·7 acres; H. D. Brown and L. Min-liang, *A Survey of Fifty Farms* (*Chinese Economic Journal*, Vol. II, No. 7), giving the average of 50 farms in Szechwan as 8·0 acres; Paul C. Hsu, *Rural Co-operation in China*, pp. 12–13, for figures showing that out of 426 members of 22 Co-operative Societies in Kiangsu, 41 per cent farmed less than 2½ acres; and Leonard S. Hsu, *Study of a Typical Chinese Town*, p. 9, for figures showing that in Chingho 64 per cent of the families farmed holdings of under 3 acres.

other relatives, who, though not forming part of the household, share the family budget. Hence the number of human beings which each of these dwarf farms must support is larger than in the West.[1] Apart from the encouragement of migration and of the settlement of unoccupied lands, no policy for increasing the size of the smallest holdings, such as has been adopted by some European Governments and has from time to time been considered in India, appears to have been carried out in China.

[1] The following figures have been supplied to me by the kindness of Chinese friends. Those in (i) relate to 5,255 families in the neighbourhood of Ting Hsien (Hopei) and represent the provisional results obtained by the Survey Department of the Mass Education Movement. Those in (ii) I owe to Dr. L. K. Tao and his colleagues of the Institute of Social Research; they relate to 12,912 families in 53 villages in the north-west part of Chekiang.

(i)		(ii)	
Persons per Family	Number of Families	Persons per Family	Number of Families
1	194	1	1,074
2	402	2	1,477
3	675	3	2,152
4	852	4	2,523
5	778	5	1,976
6	666	6	1,533
7	534	7	799
8	329	8	488
9	214	9	292
10	159	10	187
11	130	11	123
12	85	12	93
13	63	13	33
14	43	14	37
15	26	15	35
16	16	16	18
17	16	17	24
18	11	18	9
19	14	19	12
20	11	20	4
21	7	21 and over	23
22	6		
23	8	Average size, 4·6 persons per family.	
24 and over	16		
Average size, 5·8 persons per family.			

On the size of the families, see also Buck, *Chinese Farm Economy*, pp. 317 *et seq.* (where figures are given showing that the average size of 2,640 farm families in 16 localities is 5·65 persons), and Chiao and Buck, *The Composition and Growth of Rural Population Groups in China* (*Chinese Economic Journal*, Vol. II, No. 3, March, 1928).

The causes of this *morcellement* of land are not obscure. It is the natural consequence of the relation existing between resources and population. Dr. D. K. Lieu and Dr. Chung Min-chen have estimated the farm land per head of population at just over half an acre, and Professor Baker at just over a third. Industries other than agriculture, though important in themselves, are still but little developed. Owing to ignorance, strong local attachments, lack of surplus resources and bad means of communication, internal migration on a large scale has in the past been difficult. The number of Chinese living abroad is said to be between six and seven million, or less than 2 per cent of the total population,[1] and there has been nothing comparable to the vast movement of emigration which served Europe as a safety-valve in the nineteenth century. When a population as large as that of China is struggling for a foothold on an area which is already fully occupied, and which in the view of some authorities is actually contracting,[2] the multiplication of dwarf holdings is, in the absence of a deliberate policy to counteract it, the inevitable consequence. The results of economic pressure have been further intensified by the rule prescribing equal partition of property among heirs. A comparative study of the size of farms at different dates appears still to be lacking; but such evidence as has been secured suggests that in certain parts of China it has, even in the recent past, diminished.[3]

The small size of most farms is the fact from which the whole scheme of Chinese agriculture has taken its stamp. The prevalence of minute holdings has necessitated special methods of cultivation in order to make them yield a livelihood; and these methods in turn, involving, as they do, much detailed

---

[1] *Chinese Migration: Its Causes and Characteristics*, by Tsao Lien-en (*Chinese Economic Journal*, Vol. VII, No. 2, July, 1930).

[2] Owing to the destruction of forests and the advance of the desert. See, e.g., *China, the Land and the People*, by Dudley Buxton (Oxford University Press, 1929).

[3] See *The Chinese Economic Journal*, Vol. II, No. 3 (March, 1928), p. 224, where it is stated that a survey of 150 farms in Yenshan County (Hopei) shows a decrease of 14·3 per cent in the size of farms in a period of thirteen and a half years, and this though about 13 per cent of the population of the present generation has migrated.

vigilance and heavy physical labour, are of a kind which can be applied only when holdings are minute. Spontaneously, unaided by science or theory and without guidance from above, by an effort which seems at first sight as instinctive as that of the beaver, but which in reality is the expression of habits formed and experience accumulated during many centuries, the Chinese farmer has elaborated a technique which enables him, though with heavy losses and recurrent defeats, to keep starvation at bay. Cut off by his environment from the easy triumphs of extensive farming, he has acquired an ingenuity which has rarely been surpassed in wringing from the land at his disposal, not, indeed, the most that it could yield— for the output could be increased by the use of modern methods —but the utmost possible with the resources that he has hitherto commanded.

The foundations on which this technique rests are two. The first is the protection and fertilisation of the cultivable area by works originally constructed by collective effort under the direction of the Government. The second is the minute attention and patient skill of the individual cultivator. The permanent menace of the Chinese farmer is either too much water or too little. Its control is the condition of growing the rice which is the characteristic crop of the south; in large parts of the north it is the condition, not merely of prosperous agriculture, but of any agriculture at all. The celebrated system of canals, reservoirs, embankments and irrigation works, by which it was attempted to meet the need, was begun more than three thousand years ago, and was still in process of extension in the nineteenth century. If inadequate, when judged by modern standards, it is among the greatest achievements of the art of the engineer. It made possible the growth of a dense population in regions which, in its absence, would have been derelict through flood and drought, and its pioneers are among the half-legendary heroes of Chinese history.

Devices organised on a grand scale by the state, to protect whole regions, must be equally employed on a humble one by

individuals, by villages and by neighbouring communities
acting in association with each other. Dykes must be maintained, canals dredged, sluices kept in repair, crops irrigated
by streams led in channels through the fields, rice lands flooded
to the proper depth. The co-operation—and quarrelling—
which, in the European village, had their occasion in the
maintenance of the common course of cultivation, and the
regulation of the use of common pastures, meadows and
woods, by the court of the manor, in China finds its most
striking expression in the control of water; in some regions,
for example, if a canal runs through a number of villages,
each village uses it in turn by agreement, the time of use by
each farmer being regulated by the burning of an incense
stick, and the disputes being appropriately settled in the temple
of the God of War. More than in any other country, not
excepting Holland, land in China is an article manufactured
by man. If the area under irrigation and protected against
flood were extended, large numbers would live who now die;
if it contracted, the number of deaths from famine would be
even greater than it is to-day.

In this framework of the past, the peasant is compelled by
the smallness of his holding to practise an agriculture which
has been aptly described as a kind of gardening. It is the
agriculture of a pre-scientific age, raised by centuries of
venerable tradition to the dignity of an art. Compared with
that of most parts of Europe, in any period before the nineteenth century, it is a prodigy of efficiency, and, as a triumph
of individual skill unaided by organised knowledge, its reputa-
tion is deserved. Its distinctive features have so often been
analysed that it is needless to labour them. But their economic
significance has not always been appreciated, and admirers of
the technical expertness of the Chinese farmer seem sometimes
to forget the human cost at which his triumphs are won.[1] It is
possible to applaud the miracles of ingenuity performed in
coping with overwhelming difficulties, without ceasing to

[1] The well-known book of F. H. King, *Farmers of Forty Centuries*, seems to be
open to this criticism.

regret that conditions should be such as to make miracles a necessity. Yet that sentiment in its turn is liable to mislead. The criteria applied in one civilisation cannot be transferred *en bloc* to another. In China, as in Europe during long periods of its history, the ideal commonly accepted, though too rarely attained, has been, not progress, but stability. The primary concern has been, not to secure the maximum return for the minimum effort, but to distribute limited and unexpanding resources among the largest possible number of human beings.

Good farming in the West increasingly rests on chemistry, biology and mechanical invention. Except here and there, where it has been influenced by the extension work of the universities and the Government, that of China is little affected by them. Tools are primitive: a heavy hoe, a rake of bamboo or crudely wrought iron, a plough which turns up the soil to a depth of a few inches, stone rollers for levelling furrows when seeds have been sown, a long-handled sickle for cutting crops, home-made flails with which grain is threshed on a clay floor. Except in Manchuria, where tractors are increasingly employed, mechanical power is hardly used, for, even could farmers afford the capital outlay, the small size of most fields would make it impracticable. Animal power is used, indeed, but on a scale that is insignificant compared with its importance in western countries. Part of the work elsewhere performed by beasts is done by the labour of the farmer and his family.

The technique which he employs varies widely from region to region and from crop to crop, and a generalised description is necessarily misleading. The agriculture of Manchuria, with its semi-colonial conditions, is a world by itself. The farming of the north, where water is scarce, and where the principal crops are millet and wheat, contrasts sharply with the irrigated rice fields of the south. The cultivation of tea is one thing, of cotton another, of vegetables a third, while the breeding of silkworms, though carried on in conjunction with them, is a distinct art. The common factor, which gives the methods of most parts of

China such unity as they possess, is the necessity, since land is scarce, of squeezing the last ounce of nutriment out of such land as there is. It is hardly an exaggeration to say, indeed, that its deficiency is supplemented by farming water.

If economy is parsimony, economy has been turned by that necessity into the most ruthless of religions. The note of the system is economy of space, economy of materials, economy of implements, economy of fodder, economy of fuel, economy of waste products, economy of everything except of forests, which have been plundered, with prodigal recklessness, to the ruin of the soil, and of the labour of human beings, whom social habits have made abundant and abundance cheap. When natural conditions allow, land is prepared by grading it to water level, which checks waste by erosion and retains water on the fields. Fertility is conserved with an efficiency unknown, till recently, in the West, not by the use, save here and there, of artificial manures, but by what has aptly been described as farming in a circle—by the careful conservation of animal, vegetable and human refuse, and its restoration to the soil, and sometimes, indeed, by mixing it with soil before it is applied. Food for animals is saved by a lavish use of human power in the work of cultivation, in raising water with pumps worked by hand or by the feet, and in carrying on the backs of human beings instead of on beasts. Land is made more productive by systematic irrigation. Since space cannot be increased, an alternative is found in economising time, by sowing one crop between the rows of another, the first being gathered while the second is still growing. Rice is planted in seed-beds, and later transplanted by hand so as to extend the period during which the fields are in use. Double cropping, made possible by the long growing season, is common in north China and general in the south; it is said that in parts of the latter as many as four crops are sometimes raised in succession. When the last has been cut, every scrap that has been left on the ground is removed with a rake, to serve as fuel. The stubble has the appearance of having been brushed and combed.

A comparison of the yield of three crops in China and other countries is given in the following table.[1]

| | WHEAT | | CORN | | RICE | |
| | Acreage | Yield per Acre | Acreage | Yield per Acre | Acreage | Yield per Acre |
	(Millions)	(Bushels)*	(Millions)	(Bushels)†	(Millions)	(lb.)
United States ..	58·1	13·9	102·8	27·8	·9	1,076
Canada ..	22·1	16·6	—	—	—	—
England and Wales ..	1·7	32·9	—	—	—	—
France	13·5	21·5	—	—	—	—
Germany ..	3·6	27·3	—	—	—	—
Spain	13·5	13·6	—	—	—	—
Italy	11·5	17·2	3·8	24·9	—	—
Russia	39·1	10·1	5·3	17·4	—	—
India	29·6	11·4	5·9	13·9	81·4	863
Japan	—	—	—	—	7·7	2,350
Indo-China ..	—	—	—	—	11·9	643
Java and Madura	—	—	4·0	15·2	8·0	880
China	50·7	10·8	8·0	11·7	50·0	1,750

    * Bushels of 60 lb.   † Bushels of 56 lb.

It will be seen that the yield of rice per acre is higher in China than in any country except Japan, but that the yield of wheat per acre is lower in China than in any country except Russia, and that of corn the lowest of all.

It has become almost a convention to dwell on the intensiveness of cultivation in China; but the word is ambiguous. Chinese agriculture is intensive in its use of labour, unintensive in the inadequacy of the equipment by which labour is aided, and in its failure to make use of the results of science. Judged by the standards of the West, which are not necessarily final, it is at once under-capitalised and over-manned. As a consequence, in the case of rice, where its traditional methods are seen at their best, the output per acre is surprisingly high, though less high than it might be were modern knowledge

[1] All figures, except those for China, are the average of the years 1921–25, and are taken from the United States Commerce Year Book, 1929, Vol. II, pp. 702–707. Figures for China are from O. E. Baker, *op. cit.*, p. 337; figures for wheat being the average of 1914–18, corn the average of 1914–17 and rice the average of 1916–18.

utilised, and less high than it is in Japan, where conditions somewhat similar to those of China obtain; but the output per worker is invariably low. It is the latter, not the former, which determines the standard of life of the agricultural population. Prosperity is a condition, not of acres, but of human beings. The results of such an economy, if instructive to the agriculturalist, must raise doubts in the sociologist.

CHAPTER III

THE PROBLEMS OF THE PEASANT

The economy of China was for long immobile, for geography had isolated her. On the seaboard, on the rivers, and in a few great cities, it has been, since the advent of the steamship, in process of change. Change confronts her with issues similar to those which have sprung elsewhere from the Industrial Revolution, and their intelligent treatment is vital to her future. But, since three-quarters of her population live by tilling the land, by traditional handicrafts and by petty commerce, her gravest problems are of a different kind. They are those, not of an industrial, but of an agricultural, civilisation; nor must it be forgotten that the social consequences produced by capitalist industry, as is shown by its history in Europe and in America, depend partly on the character of the rural environment in which it develops. Not the wage-worker, but the peasant, is the representative figure in China to-day; and, as industrialism develops, it will be from peasant families, with the standard of life to which the farm has habituated them, that the industrial wage-workers will be drawn. Before considering, therefore, the case of the latter, it is necessary to glance at the situation of the former.

(i)

METHODS OF CULTIVATION

Those entitled to express an opinion are few, and the layman can do no more than reproduce their conclusions. Agriculture is at once a craft, a business, and a manner of life. Its problems are partly technical, partly financial and commercial, partly cultural and social. The Chinese peasant is, by general agreement, a highly skilled farmer, who has achieved, in certain branches of his art, an extraordinary efficiency. But the centuries of tradition which have perfected his technique have also narrowed it. Admirable as is his individual accomplishment, the basis of experience on which it rests is that of a single district or province, if not sometimes, indeed, a single village. Though his methods are the finest of their type, that type itself has hitherto missed the stimulus which the recent progress of agricultural science could offer it.

Hence, even in the details of daily routine, the skilful mastery of which is the special strength of Chinese agriculture, its practices are not always, if friendly observers may be trusted, according to knowledge. The choice of seeds, they point out, is not infrequently casual. In one district wheat, in another cotton, in a third silk, suffers through haphazard selection; varieties of grain suitable only for low-lying irrigated fields are sown on arid mountain slopes; when, as is often the case, the need for better strains is realised by the farmer himself, lack of credit facilities makes it impossible to obtain them; and, while trial and error have taught him the crops best suited to his locality, custom sometimes causes opportunities of introducing new departures to be missed, even when the development of fresh markets in the neighbourhood has made them profitable. Methods of sowing are still, in some districts, primitive, and weeding inadequate; in others ploughs are used which do not turn the soil to a sufficient depth. Fertility, the conservation of which is the special and, on the whole, well-founded boast of Chinese farming, is injured by the practice of stripping the land after harvest of every shred and particle of organic matter, stalks, straw, grass and leaves, to burn as a substitute for coal and wood. Plant diseases result in heavy damage—a survey made in 1925 of Shantung, Honan and northern Anhwei showed a loss through rust and smut of 16 per cent on wheat and 20 per cent on kaoliang. Veterinary science is still in its infancy. Understocking causes a deficiency of manure, which is not adequately made up by purchased fertilisers, and hampers ploughing and harrowing at the proper season.

Work is intense in certain months, but is less well distributed than, with a better combination of crops and subsidiary industries, it might be, so that, in some districts, only one hundred days a year are spent on farm employments. Though, owing to the small size of farms and cheapness of labour, no extensive use of machinery is generally practicable, yet, even where it could be used to advantage, as in pumping and threshing, it is still rarely employed. The larger matters of the arrangement of holdings and the control of the environment leave much to be desired. The scattered plots into which farms are divided involve waste of time and of labour, and hamper drainage, irrigation and the control of pests. Wells are often inadequate, both in number and in depth. Though farms are already too small, the land available for cultivation is still further diminished by the multitude of graves, often centuries old. The disastrous destruction of forests by previous generations—China is thought to have been once well wooded —diminishes the cultivable area and aggravates floods.[1]

As a consequence, the output, not merely per man, but per acre, of most crops, except rice, is lower than it is where farming is less intensive than in China, and, even in the case of rice, is not conspicuously high. If the decline in China's share in the world's output of tea and silk, and her increasing, though still small, dependence on foreign foodstuffs, are partly due to unavoidable causes, they are partly the result, good judges assert, of the persistence of methods which have had their day; and complaints are now made that the trade in

[1] For statements on the above point, see *Chinese Economic Journal*, Vol. VI, No. 3, p. 252 (Cotton Seeds); *ibid.*, No. 11, p. 17 (Silk); *ibid.*, Vol. VII, No. 3, pp. 980–991 (Seeds and Shallow Ploughing); T. S. Chu and T. Chin, *Marketing of Cotton in Hopei Province* (Bulletin No. 3, Institute of Social Research, Peiping, 1929), pp. 52–53 (Cotton); W. Y. Swen, *A Study of Types of Farming in Weihsien County, Shantung*, pp. 659–660 (Cotton and Silk); L. M. Outerbridge, *Seeds for China's Arid Areas* (*Annals*, November, 1930); Buck, *Chinese Farm Economy*, pp. 182 *et seq.*, and *China Year Book*, 1928, p. 1016 (Neglect of New Crops); *Chinese Economic Monthly*, Vol. III, No. 7 (Primitive Methods of Sowing); Swen, *op. cit.*, and Buck, *op. cit.*, p. 225 (Destruction of Fertility); Buck, *An Economic and Social Survey of 150 Farms*, p. 54 (Weeding); Tayler, *Farm and Factory in China*, p. 26, and Buck, *Chinese Farm Economy*, Ch. VIII (Distribution of Labour); Buck, *op. cit.*, pp. 23–28 (Scattered Plots); Mallory, *China, Land of Famine*, pp. 37 and 98–99 (Deforestation and Graves); W. C. Lowdermilk, *Forestry in Denuded China* (*Annals*, November, 1930).

soy beans,[1] the staple product of Manchuria, is likely to be prejudiced for similar reasons. What is more important, the income of the peasant is less than it might be. He suffers because his admirable skill and devoted labour are still too little supplemented by the resources of science.

(ii)

MARKETING

The farmer must not only sow and reap his crops; he must finance his business, market the produce and, unless he owns his holding, meet his obligations to a landlord. In countries where the family farm is the prevalent type and where capital and reserves are small, these matters are vital. In an industrial civilisation the central problem is the wage-contract; in a society of peasants, it is prices, credit and tenure. It is through the improvement of the commercial and financial organisation of agriculture, as much as by the use of better methods of production, that the progress of the last half-century in Europe has taken place.

Chinese villages are not self-sufficient units, though some larger areas are. Many articles that in the West would be bought are made at home; but, if the regions so far investigated are typical, rather more than a quarter of the goods consumed by agricultural families are purchased. Hence, farming is carried on for the market, rather than for subsistence, to a greater degree than is sometimes suggested. While the pro-

---

[1] *Chinese Economic Journal*, Vol. VII, No. 3, September, 1930, p. 967. B. P. Torgasheff, *China as a Tea Producer* (1926), pp. 76 *et seq.*: "Backward methods of cultivation, scattered holdings, lack of systematic planting, absence of capital in the hands of the farmers, complete lack of knowledge as to how to maintain the quality of tea in less-favoured years, unwillingness gradually to improve quality, all this has contributed to the rapid disintegration of the tea trade in China." Y. W. Wong, *Silk Industry in China* (Commercial Press, 1929), p. 162: "In China, 75 per cent of the silkworms hatched were killed by germs. Thus, in Japan or France, one ounce of silkworms can, if hatched, return 110–113 pounds of cocoons; in China the quantity is often reduced to only 15–25 pounds." I am indebted for a translation of the last passage to the kindness of Dr. Fong, of Nankai University.

portion of produce sold varies with differences of crop and district, it is noticeable that not only the commercial crops, such as cotton, tea, tobacco and silk, but also food crops, are raised largely for sale. The general practice appears to be for the higher-priced produce to be sold, and for the inferior to be consumed at home. It was found, for example, in a district of Shantung, that, while the kaoliang was eaten on the farm, 50 per cent of the wheat was usually exported to other places. A study of a group of 50 farmers near Chengtu indicated that they were compelled by economic stress to dispose of the greater part of their crops immediately after harvest. The more extensive researches of Professor Buck show that, on the 2,866 farms for which data were obtainable, rather more than a third of the rice, about half the wheat, beans and peas, two-thirds of the barley, and three-quarters of the sesame and vegetables, were produced for the market. Of the total output 53 per cent was disposed of off the farm.[1]

When so much of the produce is sold, the prosperity of the farmer depends on the margin between costs and price, and the margin on the character of the marketing system. The subject has not yet been adequately studied, but it is clear that the scales are somewhat heavily weighted against the producer. Except for certain limited areas, railway and motor traffic are insignificant, and, as far as the mass of peasants are concerned, might as well not exist. Apart from water, the usual means of transport are carts, mules and donkeys, especially in the north; wheelbarrows of a size which almost make them into carts propelled by men; and the shoulders of human beings. Bad communications and primitive methods make the cost of moving crops far afield almost prohibitive. Mr. Arnold has remarked that, if farmers in Shensi were to make a present of their grain to mill-owners in Shanghai, it would still pay the latter better to import grain from Seattle than to pay its freightage in China; while rice is fetching $10 in Hangchow, it is sold at $15 in the hilly regions of the same province;

[1] W. Y. Swen, *op. cit.*, pp. 647–648; H. D. Brown and Li Min-liang, *A Survey of Fifty Farms, etc.* (*Chinese Economic Journal*, Vol. II, No. 1); Buck, *op. cit.*, pp. 196–202.

wheat has been known to sell in Szechwan at barely more than one-tenth of its price on the eastern coast; in parts of the country the expense of moving it fifty miles exceeds its price in the place where it is grown.[1] As a result, there are a multitude of little localised markets, in which prices fluctuate violently with every change in the local supply, and, while consumers in one region are threatened with famine, farmers are ruined in another because they cannot dispose of their surplus. The difficulties caused by lack of tolerable communications are aggravated by internal taxes. In the eighty miles between Peiping and Tientsin, seven tax barriers were till recently passed. A cargo of soy beans sent by the producing district of Fuchin to the manufacturing district of Harbin had to pay, it is stated, no less than twenty-two separate dues.[2]

Apart from the expenses of transport, the farmer is in a weak position to drive a bargain. Owing to lack of reserves, he must often sell immediately after harvest, when the market is falling. He is ignorant of the prices ruling in other districts. Being obliged to sell to buyers in his immediate neighbourhood, he is an easy prey to the local monopolist. The dealers with whom he does business are sometimes strongly organised in a gild, which fixes prices, forbids over-bidding among its members, and, occasionally, when a market-manager—an official with duties analagous to the clerk of the market of Tudor England —is employed by the local authority licensing the market, is able to secure a voice in his appointment and to put pressure on him. The result is shown in the valuable study of certain marketing centres in north China made by Professor J. B. Tayler.[3] The price on the Chingho market of the four principal grains, wheat, millet, kaoliang and maize, rises sharply before harvest when stocks are running low, and then falls with a crash. So little affected is one market by prices in

---

[1] *Chinese Economic Journal*, Vol. VII, No. 4, October, 1930, p. 1069; *ibid.*, Vol. III, No. 10, October, 1926, pp. 437–438; Ming Ju Chen, *The Influence of Communications*, pp. 34 *et seq.*
[2] *Chinese Economic Journal*, Vol. VII, No. 3, September, 1930, pp. 964–966.
[3] I am indebted to Professor Tayler for kindly allowing me to see this in manuscript.

another, even in its immediate neighbourhood, that, though
Chingho is distant only eight miles from Peiping, the price in
the former was at times far above, at times far below, that in
the latter.

Such an environment makes it easy for a group of dealers to
corner the market. Its effects are aggravated by the fact that,
in China, seasonal variations in prices are unusually violent,
and that the sharp drop after harvest, followed by a sharp rise
a few months later, when stocks are exhausted,[1] plays into the
hands of the speculator. A good deal of what passes under the
name of trade appears to consist of the practices described in a
less polite age as forestalling and regrating. The dealer with
his larger reserves, wider sources of information and large
opportunities for combination, naturally comes off better than
the farmer. Nor are these conditions confined to the trade in
wheat. Rice, it is stated in an account of farming in western
China, is sold by the peasants immediately after harvest at $10
a picul (133·3 pounds) and re-purchased by them in spring,
when the price has risen to $28, so that the merchant makes
a profit on the transaction of between 100 and 200 per cent.
Tea, before reaching the export firms, is said to pass through
the hands of as many as ten middlemen, with the result that
a picul purchased in Anhwei for $1.50 is marketed in Shanghai
for $14.[2] The cost of marketing cotton, exclusive of profit,
from Nanking to Tientsin is stated to be 19·1 per cent, from
Shansi 21·6 per cent, and from Hantan 23·8 per cent; the
Wukiang co-operative society, founded under the auspices
of the College of Agriculture of the University of Nanking,
succeeded, by organised selling, in securing for its members
an additional profit of $5.84 per picul on ordinary cotton
and of $6.84 on improved cotton.[3] A study recently made of
the marketing of peanuts produced in Honan for Shanghai
showed that, on thirty transactions, the farmer received be-

[1] H. D. Brown and L. Min-liang, op. cit.

[2] B. P. Torgasheff, China as a Tea Producer (1926), p. 80.

[3] T. S. Chu and T. Chin, Marketing of Cotton in Hopei Province (Bulletin No. III,
Institute of Social Research, Peiping), pp. 38–41; Paul C. Hsu, Rural Co-operation
in China, p. 10.

tween one-half and two-thirds of the price paid by the consumer, and that over 16 per cent went in profits and commissions, apart from interest on capital, to the dealers. In the case of one large business, the farmers' share of the proceeds was 56·2 per cent, while profits and commissions amounted to over 30 per cent.[1]

(iii)

CREDIT

Agriculture is an industry of slow turnover. Means must be found to finance the interval between sowing and harvest, and the peasant, with his small resources, cannot normally provide them. Hence, in all countries where farming is in the hands of small producers, the fundamental problem of rural society is not that of wages, but of credit. All over Europe, from the early Middle Ages to the nineteenth century, a long wail arose against the unconscionable extortions of the damnable sect of usurers. It is only since alternative facilities for borrowing have been organised by governments and voluntary associations that the problem of protecting the peasant against the money-lender has been solved. In India, in spite of the efforts of the authorities, it is still acute.

No statistics exist as to the indebtedness of Chinese farmers, but all observers are agreed that it is always extensive and sometimes crushing. The peasant's capital is tiny, and his income too small to enable him to save. Towards the end of the winter, when last year's grain is exhausted, he is often on the verge of starvation, and any unexpected emergency drives his head under water. The gravity of the situation has been realised. In 1915 the Government of the day passed a measure for the creation of agricultural banks; several provincial governments have since that time established them; and since 1923 agricultural credit societies have been organised through the initiative of the International Famine Relief Com-

---

[1] *Chinese Economic Journal*, Vol. V, No. 3, pp. 779–781.

mission, of the agricultural departments of certain universities, and of a few provinces.[1] Their success has been striking, but the co-operative movement is in its infancy, and it is probable that its total membership does not exceed at most 100,000. Apart from its activities, and from temporary associations for mutual assistance, formed here and there, as need arises, by the peasants themselves,[2] the financing of agriculture is casual and unsystematic. As is usual in such circumstances, it is extravagantly expensive.

The principal purposes for which capital is required by the farmer are three, though no clear division between them is applicable to China—permanent improvements, such as the making of wells and drains; expenditure on intermediate needs, such as livestock and implements; and current requirements. No organised machinery, such as the loans at low rates of interest from public funds that are available in some countries, exist for the first. Improvements are made piecemeal out of current income, by extra labour on the part of the farmer himself, or by the hire of temporary assistance to meet an urgent need, sometimes with the help of his landlord, if he has one. His need for intermediate and short-term credit,[3] if the

[1] For details, see China International Famine Relief Commission, Series B, No. 37 (*Herr Raiffeisen among Chinese Farmers*, 1930); Paul C. Hsu, *Rural Co-operation in China*; Chunjen C. C. Chen, *Agricultural Co-operative Movement in China* (*China Critic*, July 4 and 11, 1929); Chi-lieu Hsu, *Rural Credit in China* (*Chinese Social and Political Science Review*, Vol. VII, Nos. 1 and 2); *Chinese Economic Bulletin*, Vol. XIII, No. 7, July 7, 1928, for an agricultural bank in Chekiang; *ibid.*, No. 22, December 1, 1928, and Vol. XII, No. 11, March 17, 1928, for banks in Hupeh and Shantung.

[2] For accounts of such arrangements, see *Chinese Economic Bulletin*, Vol. XII, No. 22, June 2, 1928; F. C. H. Lee and T. Chin, *Village Families in the Vicinity of Peiping*, p. 25; D. K. Lieu, *China's Industries and Finance*, pp. 51–52; Buck, *An Economic and Social Survey of 150 Farms*, etc., p. 90; and for an earlier description, A. H. Smith, *Village Life in China*, Chapter 14.

[3] Some idea of the relative importance of these different types of credit may be gathered from the purposes to which the loans made to co-operative societies by the China International Famine Relief Commission are applied. According to the report (*Herr Raiffeisen among Chinese Farmers*, 1930, p. 34), of the loans made in 1929, 29 per cent was used for grain, seed, fodder, cultivating expenses, etc.; 30·3 per cent for buying carts, animals, implements and repairing houses; 0·6 per cent for dykes, irrigation and drainage; 1·5 per cent for social expenses, marriages, funerals, etc.; 23·4 per cent for paying off debts, and 15 per cent for other purposes, including village industries.

terms may be used, is always urgent. Unless exceptionally fortunate, he requires it every year and, in a considerable number of cases, throughout the year. He gets it where he can, when he can, on what terms he can. Since his necessities are desperate, he is often skinned alive.

Money-lending in China is a world in itself, which cries out for investigation. Whether it is to be described, in the mediaeval phrase, as a *vorago iniquitatis*, or as part of the sensitive and delicate mechanism of credit, is a matter of taste. Officials and gentry are one element in it; merchants a second; professional money-lenders, who specialise in the business, a third; pawn-shops, a vast and powerful vested interest supported by all three, a fourth; certain types of bank a fifth; farmers who have managed to lay by a little money and use it to make advances, for a consideration, to their poorer neighbours, a sixth. The ramifications of the system are endless; in Shanghai the existence of one hundred and seventy-three pawnshops—to mention only one element in it—was recently reported, ranging from considerable establishments, with a capital of $100,000, receiving valuable jewellery and furs, to humble undertakings making loans for a maximum of four months at interest of 6 per cent per month. It is stated that in Hankow there were till a few years ago over four hundred money-lenders doing pawnbrokers' business, who were organised in a gild, and charged interest up to 60 per cent, part being deducted in advance.[1]

Some farmers deal with money-lenders in large cities; but what matters to the great majority of them is the arrangements obtaining in rural districts. The principal rural money-lenders are landowners, merchants and dealers, and, though to a less extent, pawnshops. The peasant needs a loan for the work of his farm or for personal needs, to increase the stock or equip-ment of his holding, to tide over the months before his crops are sold, or to meet the temporary crisis of a wedding or

[1] *Chinese Economic Journal*, Vol. VI, No. 4, April, 1930 (*Shanghai Pawnshops and their Business Practices*); *Chinese Economic Monthly*, Vol. II, No. 8, May, 1925 (*Pawnshops in China*); *Chinese Economic Bulletin*, Vol. XI, p. 66 (Tsingtao), p. 159 (Hankow), p. 345 (Foochow); Vol. XII, pp. 79–80 (Peiping).

funeral. He gets it sometimes from the dealer to whom his crops are sold, sometimes from his landlord, sometimes from a pawnshop. Customs as to mortgaging of land, the security preferred by lenders, vary from place to place; the land may be pledged, and possession retained by the owner, or it may be temporarily transferred to the mortgagee who takes the produce as his interest. In some districts he can foreclose immediately the term of the loan expires; in others he has no remedy as long as interest continues to be paid.

The commonest form of short credit is probably a loan on crops. The farmer gets ready money before harvest, when his resources are at their lowest, by pledging his prospective crop of rice or wheat, or by selling it outright to a merchant before it is cut, at a heavy discount. Sometimes, if his means allow, he pursues a different policy, but one which also involves recourse to the money-lender. Instead of selling immediately after harvest, when prices are falling, he holds his crop back for a rise, and raises money on it in the interval; in one district a single pawnshop is said to have advanced money on rice to the amount of $40,000 to $60,000. Usually, however, his necessities are too pressing to permit of his waiting till the market recovers. He borrows on his crops at the earliest moment possible, and trusts to a favourable harvest to enable him to repay. The procedure followed in financing small farmers who cultivate cotton in Hopei, it is stated, is for well-to-do families to lend money to cotton dealers, who divide the loans into small sums and use them to make advances to the producers. The rate charged by the original lender is 12 per cent; the rate paid by the farmer is anything from 36 to 60 per cent. The legal maximum, it may be remarked, is 20 per cent, or two and half times that fixed in England by the Act of 1572.[1]

[1] For methods of borrowing and their results, see Chang Ching Yi, *The Economic Pressure on the Chinese Peasantry (Far Eastern Miscellany*, May 10, 1929); Paul C. Hsu, *op. cit.*; *Chinese Economic Bulletin*, November 5, 1927, and June 2, 1928; *Chinese Economic Monthly*, Vol. II, No. 8, August, 1925 (*Agricultural Practices in Shansi*); *ibid.*, Vol. III, No. 7, July, 1926 (*Agriculture in Kwangtung Province*); *ibid.*, No. 10, October, 1926 (*Tenancy and Land Ownership in Chekiang* and *Agricultural*

Some of these transactions are, doubtless, harmless or beneficial. It is not open to question, however, that rural indebtedness is among the curses of China. The characteristic feature of the system, and a feature which, if almost inevitable as things are to-day, is in itself vicious, is that neither borrower nor lender appears to make any clear distinction between loans needed to finance the business of farming, and loans sought to eke out the domestic budget. Everything goes down, so to speak, in a common account, with the result that there is no discrimination in the mind of either debtor or creditor between the borrowing and advancing of money for productive purposes, which should yield a return sufficient to meet the interest, and household expenses, which ought, in the absence of exceptional misfortune, to be met out of income.

In such circumstances, the rates at which loans are made naturally tend to be exorbitant. In reality, indeed, no market rate can be said to exist. The devouring of widows' houses, though in all countries a lucrative form of enterprise, is one not easily described in terms of economic theory. What the peasant pays is dictated by his necessities, and by the ability of the lender to take advantage of them. A "good money-lender," described as a blessing to his village, has been known to charge only 25 per cent; but such self-restraint is exceptional. Interest at 40 to 80 per cent is said to be common; interest at 150 to 200 per cent to be not unknown. Goods pledged are taken at two-thirds of their true value. As far as the poorer peasants are concerned, permanent indebtedness is the rule rather than the exception. They pawn their crops in summer, their farm implements in winter, and their household belongings throughout the whole twelve months. In one village in the neighbourhood of Peiping it was found that forty-four out of one hundred families borrowed in the course of the year, and in another twenty-three out of sixty-four, the average indebtedness being $31 in the first case and $68 in the

second.[1] A village of one hundred persons may owe $3,000
to its richest inhabitant, the local grain dealer, and pay
$900 a year in interest or, perhaps, $40 per family, out of
incomes not exceeding $150 a year. An exceptionally good
harvest is regarded as a doubtful blessing, since it is the
occasion for the money-lender to call in his debts. The occurrence of forced sales is, in such conditions, inevitable. Next
to drought, inability to meet the claims of the money-lender
is stated, in parts of the country, to be the principal cause of
the ruin of peasant families.

(iv)

LAND TENURE

The question of land tenure is less important in China than
that of credit. If the estimates commonly accepted are correct,
more than half her farmers are peasant proprietors. She possesses no landed aristocracy, no dominant class of *junkers* or
squires, and few beasts. She is not afflicted by the complicated
iniquities of feudal land law; manorial estates worked by
corvées, if they ever existed, have left few traces; since animal
husbandry is of secondary importance, the conflict over the
use of common pastures and meadows, which kept European
villages simmering for over a thousand years, presents no
problem. Landlord and tenant are parties to a business contract, not members of different classes based on privilege and
subordination. Hence, though questions of land tenure are in
some regions acute, their character and setting are not those
of Europe. If Chinese peasants could draft to-morrow the
cahiers des doléances—the schedules of grievances and demands
—which the deputies took to Paris in 1789, few denunciations
of servile dues and customs, *banalités*, *lods et ventes*, game laws,
and other antiquated extortions, would figure in their complaints. Attempts to apply to the land system of China analogies

[1] F. C. H. Lee and T. Chin, *Village Families in the Vicinity of Peiping* (Peiping,
1929), pp. 24–25 and 58.

derived from the past history of the West are commonly based on a misconception of both. Policies founded upon them have naturally broken down.

To say this is not to say much. It is probable that not less than thirty million farmers are, not owners, but tenants, and small landlords are not necessarily more complacent than large. China may be divided, in the matter of land tenure, into three distinct areas, the north, the south, and the regions beyond the Great Wall, Manchuria and Mongolia. In the first, where two-thirds to three-quarters of the peasants are thought to be occupying owners, the question affects only a minority of the population, though it must be remembered that, in the vast area of a Chinese province, conditions prevailing in one part of it are reversed in another. In the second region tenants, and those who, while owning some land, rent the remainder, are in a majority; if the figures of the Department of Agriculture and Commerce may be trusted, farmers so situated form 65 per cent of the agricultural households in Fukien, 66 per cent in Kwangtung, and 80 per cent in Hunan, while other evidence shows that in certain districts the proportion of tenants is as high as 90 per cent.[1] In the provinces and administrative districts north of the Great Wall, into which a fresh flood of immigrants pours every year, conditions are still too fluid, perhaps, to admit of generalisation. It is known, however, that, side by side with much small ownership, large tracts of land have been acquired, sometimes by methods of doubtful propriety, by officials and military adventurers, and are leased to tenant farmers, often for a rent which, in the first instance, is nominal, but which is subsequently raised.[2] In such circumstances, the complacent dismissal of the question of land tenure as irrelevant to the conditions of China is hardly justified. It is of secondary, though of increasing, importance

[1] See above, pp. 34–37.
[2] The figures of ownership and tenancy in the three provinces of Liaoning, Kirin and Heilungkiang were stated to be in 1927 as follows: total number of farms, 2,549,704; owners, 1,118,642 (43·8 per cent); tenants, 728,187 (28·6 per cent); part owners renting land from others, 702,875 (27·6 per cent). See *China Year Book*, 1928, pp. 111–112, where the conditions prevailing among them are described.

in the north. It is serious in the south. In ten years' time, whatever the political future of the north-eastern provinces, it may be serious in Manchuria.

The part played by custom in determining the relations between landlord and tenant has already been mentioned. At one end of the scale are peasants who, in their security against rack-renting and eviction, and their freedom to dispose as they please of their tenant-right, may be described, perhaps, as customary free-holders. At the other end of it are peasants who hold at will, pay a rent fixed by verbal agreement and liable to be increased at the landlord's pleasure, can be summarily dispossessed without compensation, save for permanent improvements, cannot transfer their interest to a third party, are, in some cases, it appears, actually required by their tenure to perform labour-services for their landlords, and, when tension is acute, are terrorised by the latter by the use of armed force. The great mass of tenants occupy a position between the two, with rights and obligations varying from district to district. In the matter of payment for their holdings, they fall into two principal groups, each of which, however, has numerous sub-divisions. The first consists of *métayers*, who hold by some form of share tenancy, paying a proportion of their crops to the landlord, in return for his providing them with part of their seed, manure, livestock and equipment; the second, of those who pay a stipulated rent, reckoned either in money, in produce or in produce converted into terms of cash.[1]

Over-renting is a grievance of long standing in certain parts of China, and protests on the subject were, from time to time, addressed to the Government under the old régime.[2] Such

[1] *China Year Book*, 1928, pp. 1015–16; Chang Ching Yi, *op. cit.*; Buck, *Farm Ownership and Tenancy in China*; T. C. Chang, *The Farmers' Movement in Kwangtung* (National Christian Council of China, 1928); Agnes Smedley, *Peasants and Landlords in China* (*New Republic*, September 3, 1930).

[2] See, e.g., *Tenure of Land in China and the Condition of the Rural Population* in the *Journal* of the China Branch of the Royal Asiatic Society for 1888, New Series, Vol. XXIII, p. 64: "The rents have been raised from time to time till the cultivators have been reduced to a state of abject poverty. Their deplorable conditions, and the impossibility of collecting the rents, have been the subject of various memorials from the viceroy of Chihli in recent years."

recent estimates as have been made of the distribution of the proceeds between tenant and landlord suggest that the proportion taken by the latter is, in some parts of the country at least, surprisingly high. Rents are said to absorb approximately 50 per cent of the produce in parts of Hupeh, 55 per cent in parts of Kiangsu, between 50 and 60 per cent in parts of Hunan, and 55 to 66 per cent on small farms in Kwangtung. A sample study[1] of tenancy recently made gives the following figures of the percentage of the yield taken by the landlord under (i) the share-rent system, by which he shares the risk with the tenant and receives a fixed proportion of the crop, whatever the latter may be, and (ii) the crop-rent system, by which he receives a payment in kind stipulated in advance:

	Superior Grade Per cent	Medium Grade Per cent	Inferior Grade Per cent
(i) *Share-Rent*			
Irrigated land	52	48	45
Non-irrigated land ..	48	45	44
(ii) *Crop-Rent*			
Irrigated land	46·3	46·2	45·8
Non-irrigated land ..	45·3	44·6	44·4

The percentage which the third type of rent, cash-rent, formed of the price of the land, and therefore the landlord's return on his outlay, was as follows:

	Superior Grade Per cent	Medium Grade Per cent	Inferior Grade Per cent
(iii) *Cash-Rent*			
Irrigated land	10·3	11·3	12·0
Non-irrigated land ..	10·5	10·9	12·0

These figures indicate that the tenant pays about half his crops to the landlord for the use of the land, and that the landlord gets interest at about 11 per cent. Statistics collected by Professor Buck point to the same conclusion. Though they relate to districts in which the commercialisation of land-tenure has proceeded less far than in the south, they show that the proportion of the total receipts paid to the landlord on 641 farms varied from 24·6 to 66·6 per cent, and on the

[1] C. C. Chang, *Farm Tenancy in China* (*China Critic*, September 30, 1930). See also *Chinese Economic Journal*, Vol. I, No. 2, February, 1927 (*Agriculture in Hupeh*); *China Year Book*, 1928, pp. 1013–18.

farms in seven villages out of twelve exceeded 40 per cent.[1]
The interest received by him on his investment averaged 8·4
per cent. Compared with the extortions of the money-lender,
the figure is low; but, in the scramble for land which goes on,
holdings can always be re-let, and the security is as nearly
gilt-edged as is possible in China. The reasonableness of the
rent depends partly, of course, on the extent to which the
landlord assists the farmer with capital and shares his risks.
Professor Buck's own conclusion is that, if a fair rent be interpreted as one which results in the division of receipts between
tenant and landlord in the proportion in which each contri-
butes to the expenses, the tenant is getting too little and the
landlord too much.

The phenomenon is usually, no doubt, a smaller evil than
the inability of the farmer to get the best price for his produce,
and his exploitation by the money-lender; but, in view of the
tiny income of most Chinese peasants, it is sufficiently serious.
It is probably understated, since conditions are more favourable to tenants in the north than in the south. The reality of
the grievance is admitted by the authorities; successive conferences of the Kuomintang have passed resolutions in favour
of a general reduction of rents, and the land policy of the
Government is understood to include the establishment of
machinery to fix rents with a view to the protection of tenants.[2]
Nor is over-renting the only aspect of the problem. Owing to
the multitude of small proprietors tilling their own holdings,
property in land has been less important as a factor in class
stratification in China than, for many centuries, it was in
Europe; and, in most parts of the country, the owners of the
soil, as distinct from its cultivators, have not formed a separate
group with a common interest and policy. In so far, however,
as absenteeism becomes common, the position is altered.
What appears to be occurring, in some regions at least, is the
emergence, side by side with small landlords who live in their
villages and are partners with their tenants in the business of

---

[1] Buck, *Chinese Farm Economy*, p. 148, and for what follows, pp. 145-46.
[2] See below, pp. 83-84, 98-99.

farming, of a class of absentee owners whose connection with agriculture is purely financial.

This development naturally proceeds most rapidly in the neighbourhood of great cities, in districts where the static conditions of rural life are broken up by the expansion of commerce and industry, and in regions like parts of Manchuria, which have recently been settled by an immigrant population. The symptoms accompanying it are land speculation, and the intrusion between landlord and tenant of a class of middlemen. In Kwangtung, it is stated, it is increasingly the practice for large blocks of land to be rented by well-to-do merchants, or even by companies especially formed for the purpose, and then to be sub-let piecemeal at a rack rent to peasant farmers. Elsewhere, a result of the growth of absentee ownership is the employment of agents, who relieve the landlord of the business of himself squeezing his tenants, browbeat the tenants by threats of eviction into paying more than they owe, and make money out of both by cheating the former and intimidating the latter. In southern Kiangsu, it was recently reported, landlords combined to maintain an office which acts as an intermediary between them and their tenants, selecting the latter, seeing that rents are paid at the proper terms, setting in motion, when payments are in arrears, the machinery for eviction, and, with the connivance of the authorities, actually detaining defaulters in a private prison and inflicting physical punishment on them.[1] Nor must it be forgotten that the landlord has often a double hold on the tenant, since the former is frequently the money-lender to whom the latter is in debt.

The growth of counter-organisation among peasants, with demands for a 25 per cent reduction of rents, the abolition of usury, establishment of provincial banks to make loans at low rates of interest, and freedom of combination—not to mention the more violent eruptions in Hunan and Kiangsi—is, in such circumstances, inevitable.[2] In parts of the country, the pay-

[1] Buck, *Farm Ownership and Tenancy in China*, pp. 18–25.
[2] T. C. Chang, *op. cit.*; Ta Chen, *Labor in China during the Civil Wars* (*Monthly Labor Review*, July, 1930, Bureau of Labor Statistics, U.S.A. Department of

ment of rent is being refused; landlords have been driven from their homes; titles have been burned, as in 1381 and 1789; and owners of holdings in excess of three hundred mow (45 acres) have been required to hand over their property above that figure to the local peasants' association for distribution among the poorer farmers. The theory that agitation is produced by agitators, not agitators by agitation, is among the western doctrines which certain circles in China have absorbed without difficulty. But no reference to communist propaganda is required to explain the no-rent campaigns and peasants' revolts which have taken place in parts of the country. It is surprising, indeed, that they have not been more frequent.

(v)

POVERTY, WAR AND FAMINE

These social conditions act on a society in which the standard of life of the mass of the population is already depressed by economic forces. The latter are ultimately the more important, but the former intensify them. No comprehensive evidence exists as to the pecuniary income of Chinese farmers, and the scraps of evidence available can be briefly summarised. The most extensive survey was that made by the International Famine Relief Commission in 1922, which covered two hundred and forty villages, with 7,079 families containing 37,191 members, in the five provinces of Hopei, Kiangsu, Shantung, Anhwei and Chekiang.[1] It found that 17·6 per cent of the

---

Labor); *China Labor Year Book*, Vol. II, p. 125, where figures are given showing the total membership of farmers' unions, 1925–26, and the demands for agrarian legislation are summarised; *China Year Book*, 1928, pp. 1012–13. Owing to official repression, the membership of farmers' unions has since then diminished. I am indebted to Dr. Fong, of Nankai University, for kindly translating the relevant passages in the *China Labor Year Book*.

[1] For an account of the results of this inquiry, see J. B. Tayler, *A Study of Chinese Rural Economy* (*Chinese Social and Political Science Review*, Vol. VII, Nos. 1 and 2, January and April, 1924). As elsewhere in this study, unless otherwise stated, the dollars are Mexican dollars, equal at par to 1s. 3d. It is possible that the incomes are somewhat understated.

families in the eastern villages, and 62·2 per cent of those in the northern, had incomes of less than $50 a year. An inquiry made by Mr. Lee and Mr. Chin into two villages in the neighbourhood of Peiping showed that, in one of them, thirty-four out of one hundred families had incomes of less than $100, and thirty-nine of over $100 but less than $200, while, in the other, fifteen out of sixty-four families had less than $100 and eighteen more than $100 but less than $200.[1] The investigations of Professor Buck into the conditions prevailing among farmers in nine villages in north, and eight in east-central, China, yield somewhat similar results. In the former, the median income of the families studied was $131.08; in two out of the nine villages it was less than $100, and in three over $100 but less than $150. In the latter, the median income was $213.6; in one village it was under $200, and in three over $200 but less than $250. The average income per individual in the first group was $36.22, and in the second $68.17.[2]

More than one attempt has been made to estimate the minimum income needed to support a family in China. Professor Dittmer, on the basis of an investigation into the budgets of two hundred families in the neighbourhood of Peiping, put it in 1918 at $100. Professor Tayler, who supervised the inquiry made by the International Famine Relief Commission, put it at $150, an estimate which is accepted by Mr. Mallory.[3] If the latter figure be adopted, more than half the families in the eastern villages then examined, and more than four-fifths in the northern, had an income below the minimum required to support life. In five out of the seventeen villages studied by Professor Buck, the median income fell below the same figure.

Evidence so limited, though the best obtainable, does not, it is obvious, carry one far. On the other hand, it is known that the minute size of holdings, which is one fundamental cause of

[1] F. C. H. Lee and T. Chin, *Village Families in the Vicinity of Peiping*, pp. 23, 53.
[2] Buck, *Chinese Farm Economy*, pp. 82–89.
[3] Tayler, *op. cit.*; and Mallory, *China, Land of Famine*, pp. 9–11.

low agricultural incomes, is a phenomenon found in all parts of China, except the three north-eastern provinces. Mere acreage, it is true, is not the only point to be considered. Types of climate and soil, methods of cultivation, and social habits are also important. The rural population of Japan, where farms are no larger than in China, has a higher standard of life; and the quality of farming in China, both in its technique and business organisation, is capable of improvement. But the small area of land at the disposal of more than half the peasants in China is undoubtedly, in itself, a cruel disability. Dr. Lieu and Dr. Chung Min-chen[1] have calculated that, in China as a whole, three mow of land (0·45 acres) per person, or 2·25 acres per family of five individuals, is required to supply the bare requirements of food alone, irrespective of housing, farm equipment, clothing, fuel and other necessities. The figures published by the Department of Agriculture and Commerce in 1917 showed that 36 per cent of the farms in China were under ten mow (1·5 acres) and another 26 per cent from ten to twenty-nine mow (4·3 acres).[2] If they may be accepted, as in view of other evidence seems probable, as approximately correct, between 40 and 50 per cent of the peasant families in China have land insufficient, on the estimate of Dr. Lieu and Dr. Chung Min-chen, to provide them with food, apart from all their other requirements. The very high percentage which food absorbs of the family expenditure, the almost complete absence of meat from the diet of most agricultural families, the low standards of housing, the fact that the size of the family is plainly limited by the size of the holding and declines with the decline of the latter, the prevalence of ill-health, and the high rate both of general and infantile mortality in such districts as have been investigated, point in the same direction. There is even some reason to believe that, with the increased pressure on the land caused by the growth of population, the condition of the rural popula-

[1] D. K. Lieu and Chung Min-chen, *Statistics of Farm Land in China* (*Chinese Economic Journal*, Vol. II, No. 3, March, 1928, pp. 212–13). Their figure of three mow is an average for the whole country, four mow being required in the north and two in the south.   [2] See above, pp. 40 *et seq.*

tion, in some parts of China, may be actually worse than it was two centuries ago.[1]

Exaggeration is easy. Privation is one thing, poverty to the point of wretchedness—*la misère*—another. A sturdy and self-reliant stock may grow in a stony soil. But, when due allowance has been made for the inevitable misconceptions, it is difficult to resist the conclusion that a large proportion of Chinese peasants are constantly on the brink of actual destitution. They are, so to say, a propertied proletariat, which is saved—when it is saved—partly by its own admirable ingenuity and fortitude, partly by the communism of the Chinese family, partly

[1] For expenditure on food and for diet, see F. C. H. Lee and T. Chin, *op. cit.*, pp. 28–30 (eighty-seven out of one hundred families reported no expenditure on meat); Buck, *op. cit.*, Chapters X and XI, and *An Economic and Social Survey of 150 Farms*, pp. 74–80 (only fifteen out of one hundred and fifty farmers bought any meat during the year). For housing, see Tayler, *op. cit.*, p. 210: "If we take two persons per room as the limit between sufficient accommodation and overcrowding . . . the overcrowding in Chinhsien and Icheng would seem to exceed 90 per cent, to be in the neighbourhood of 50 per cent in Kiangyin and of 20 per cent in Wukiang"; For health and mortality no reliable figures are available, but see C. H. Chao, *A Study on the Rural Population of China*, Department of Agriculture and Forestry, University of Nanking, 1928, summarised in *Nankai Weekly Statistical Service*, March 17, 1930; Paul C. Fugh, *Reconstruction of the Chinese Elementary School Curriculum* (*Chinese Social and Political Science Review*, Vol. IX, No. 4), where the death-rate of children under five years, in Chinese and missionary families, is compared; the figures of infantile mortality given by Dr. Lenox (*China Journal of Arts and Sciences*, Vol. II, No. 5) on the basis of a study of 4,000 patients in the Peiping Union Medical College; C. M. Chiao and J. Lossing Buck, *The Composition and Growth of Rural Population Groups in China* (*Chinese Economic Journal*, Vol. II, No. 3, March, 1928), where the average death-rate for the regions studied is given as 27·9 per thousand of population, and the infantile death-rate at 254 per thousand births. For the relation between the size of families and size of holdings, see Tayler, *op. cit.*, pp. 234–5 ("In Chihli the falling off in the size of the family on the small holdings . . . is very marked, a clear indication of economic pressure"); and the following provisional figures collected by the Survey Department, Ting Hsien:

Size of Farm			Number of Families	Number of Persons	Persons per Family
Under 10 mow	..		174	823	4·7
10–29	..	..	167	1,071	6·4
30–49	..	..	76	593	7·8
50–69	..	..	43	453	10·5
70–99	..	..	37	398	10·7
100–149	..	..	10	138	13·8
150–299	..	..	8	95	11·8
Total	..		515	3,571	6·9

by reducing its consumption of necessaries and thus using up its physical capital. "The small incomes," to quote the most distinguished foreign authority on Chinese agriculture, "reduce most of the farmers and their families to a mere subsistence basis. In fact the people feed themselves in winter, just as one 'roughs' labour animals through the winter, by consuming as little and as poor food as possible."[1]

A population which has no reserves is helpless against calamity. Calamity is more frequent in China than in the West, even when allowance is made for the different form which it assumes in the latter. It is occasioned partly by civil disorder. Here again, it is necessary to avoid exaggeration. An English Chief Justice once described the special failing of his fellow-countrymen as robbery under arms. The slaughter of combatants in China is not comparable to that of the years 1914–1918 in Europe. The miseries inflicted on the civil population, though shocking, are probably less atrocious than those which accompanied the Thirty Years' War.

It is true, however, that, over a large area of China, the rural population suffers horribly through the insecurity of life and property. It is taxed by one ruffian who calls himself a general, by another, by a third, and, when it has bought them off, still owes taxes to the Government; in some places actually more than twenty years' taxation has been paid in advance. It is squeezed by dishonest officials. It must cut its crops at the point of the bayonet, and hand them over without payment to the local garrison, though it will starve without them. It is forced to grow opium in defiance of the law, because its military tyrants can squeeze heavier taxation from opium than from rice or wheat, and make money, in addition, out of the dens where it is smoked. It pays blackmail to the professional bandits in its neighbourhood; or it resists, and, a year later, when the bandits have assumed uniform, sees its villages burned to the ground.

There is a case, no doubt, for the bandit, though it is seldom stated. He is often a disbanded soldier who, as in the England

[1] Buck, *An Economic and Social Survey of 150 Farms*, p. 95.

of More, is driven "either to starve or manfully to play the thief," or a victim of oppression who robs his robbers. Unfortunately, it is easier to shear sheep than wolves, and, though popular sympathy is sometimes with him, the majority of his victims are worse off than himself. It is not surprising that, in certain provinces, the peasants have armed and formed leagues to keep out "bandits, communists and government soldiers." Much that the press ascribes to communist machinations seems, indeed, to the western observer to have as much, or as little, connection with theoretical communism as the Peasants' Revolt of 1381 in England or the *Jacquerie* in France. What is called the communist question is in reality, in most parts of the country, either a land question or a question of banditry provoked by lack of employment. It appears to be true, nevertheless, that in China, as elsewhere, an elemental revolt against intolerable injustices has been organised and given a doctrinal edge by political missionaries, and that certain regions, such as parts of Fukien, Kiangsi and Hunan—the last two areas with an abnormally high percentage of tenants, and acute agrarian discontent—form *enclaves* of revolution, where such government as exists is conducted by communists. The revolution of 1911 was a bourgeois affair. The revolution of the peasants has still to come. If their rulers continue to exploit them, or to permit them to be exploited, as remorselessly as hitherto, it is likely to be unpleasant. It will not, perhaps, be undeserved.

The indirect effects of the chaos are as disastrous as the direct. Expenditure on war absorbs resources which should be spent on elementary improvements, such as roads and primary education. Trade is paralysed, and such communications as exist are turned by the soldiers who seize them from a blessing into a curse. Capital flies from rural districts, where it is urgently needed, to be buried in the Concessions. Population flies with it; here and there whole villages are on the move, like animals breaking from cover as the beaters advance. When human enemies are absent, the farmer must still reckon with a remorseless nature. "What drove you to settle here, so far from home?" a peasant was asked in the presence of the writer. The reply was, "Bandits, soldiers and famine."[1]

Famine is the feature of Chinese economic life of which the West hears most. It is an evil so appalling that all other issues seem, at first sight, trivial. The facts have been described by skilled observers, and it is needless to labour them. Such historical evidence as is available shows that distress caused by flood and drought, on a scale sufficiently large to attract public attention, has been a recurrent feature of Chinese history. As long ago as 1878, statistics compiled by Sir Alexander Hosie[2] from Chinese records showed that, in the thousand years between 620 and 1619, drought was reported in one part of the country or another at intervals of eight to twelve years—the provinces most frequently affected by it being those of the north and centre. Mr. Ta Chen[3] has published similar figures for the sixteenth and seventeenth centuries, and has shown that emigration has been related to the occurrence of exceptional distress in China. Dr. Co-ching Chu[4] has continued the record down to the present century. His figures show that, in the two hundred and fifty-six years between 1644 and 1900, there were three provinces in which

[1] The following provisional figures, collected by the Survey Department, Ting Hsien, give some idea, though an imperfect one, of the direct economic losses caused to a group of villages by civil war alone:

LOSSES OF SIXTY-TWO VILLAGES BY CIVIL WAR IN 1928

	Extra Taxation	Looting	Total
	$	$	$
Total losses	71,733	39,862	111,595
Loss per village ..	1,157	643	1,800
Loss per family ..	6.8	3.8	10.6

Forty out of the sixty-two villages were looted during the war of 1928, involving a total loss of $39,862, or $996.5 per village looted. Four hundred and thirty-five families were affected, and suffered an average loss of $91.6 per family. The number of livestock taken by soldiers was 342, valued at $20,519. In 1927, 7,674 families in the sixty-two villages suffered losses from civil war, estimated to amount to $20,160, or $2.6 per family and $325.2 per village.

[2] For Hosie's figures and on the whole subject, see Mallory, China, Land of Famine, p. 38.

[3] Ta Chen, Chinese Migrations with Special Reference to Labour Conditions (Washington, 1928).

[4] Co-ching Chu, Climatic Pulsations in Historic Times in China (Geographical Review, April, 1926).

flood occurred more than once in every three years, three in which it occurred more than once in every four, and three in which it occurred more than once in every five. Reports of drought were somewhat less frequent. It is stated to have occurred in one province at intervals of less than four years, in two at intervals of less than seven, and in two at intervals of less than nine. The four provinces which were the principal victims of floods, namely Chihli (now Hopei), Shantung, Kiangsu and Anhwei, were also those which suffered most severely from drought. If the figures could be trusted, they would indicate that floods were somewhat, and droughts considerably, more frequent in the two and a half centuries from 1644 to 1900 than in those preceding them. But the evidence as to the later is fuller, no doubt, than for the earlier period. All that can be reasonably inferred from it is that there has been no visible improvement.

The number of deaths caused by famine has been variously estimated. That of 1849 is said to have destroyed 13,750,000 persons; the Taiping Rebellion, with the widespread economic ruin which accompanied it, 20,000,000; the famine of 1878–79, 9,000,000 to 13,000,000; that of 1920–21, 500,000. In reality, however, to concentrate attention on these sensational catastrophes, as though life ran smoothly in the intervals between them, is to misconceive the situation. Famine is a matter of degree; its ravages are grave long before its symptoms become sufficiently shocking to arouse general consternation. If the meaning of the word is a shortage of food on a scale sufficient to cause widespread starvation, then there are parts of the country from which famine is rarely absent. In Shensi, stated an eminent Chinese official at the beginning of 1931, 3,000,000 persons had died of hunger in the last few years, and the misery had been such that 400,000 women and children had changed hands by sale. In Kansu, according to Mr. Findlay Andrew, one-third of the population has died since 1926, owing to famine, civil war, banditry and typhus.[1]

[1] Speech of Mr. Yu Yu-jan, Chairman of the Control Yuan, reported in the *Peking and Tientsin Times*, January 21, 1931; and G. Findlay Andrew, *Manchester Guardian Weekly*, November 21, 1930

There are districts in which the position of the rural population is that of a man standing permanently up to the neck in water, so that even a ripple is sufficient to drown him. The loss of life caused by the major disasters is less significant than the light which they throw on the conditions prevailing even in normal times over considerable regions.

In the case of famine, in short, as in that of war, the occasion of the breakdown must be distinguished from its causes. The former is commonly a failure of crops caused by drought or flood. The latter, though aggravated at present by political anarchy, consist in the primitive organisation, and absence of surplus resources over daily needs, which turn the misfortune of individuals into a general catastrophe.[1] It is probable that drought, if not flood, is in some measure unavoidable; there are regions in the north-west where, there is reason to believe, the desert may be advancing and progressive desiccation taking place. But one reason, at least, for the occurrence of both on a scale sufficient to produce disaster is that nature has not been subjected to control to the extent which, given a settled economic policy, and the means to carry it out, is to-day practicable. Those directly affected by them cannot meet the blow, for they have no reserves. The individual cannot be rescued by his neighbours, since whole districts together are in the same position. The district cannot be rescued by the nation, because means of communication do not permit of food being moved in sufficient quantities. Famine is, in short, the last stage of a disease which, though not always conspicuous, is always present.

[1] See Mallory, *op. cit.*, p. 14.

CHAPTER IV

THE POSSIBILITIES OF RURAL PROGRESS

The problems presented by the economic conditions of rural life in China are of two principal types. There are those, in the first place, which spring from natural or inherited disadvantages, such as poverty or exhaustion of soil, a deficient or irregular rainfall, the destruction of forests, rivers liable to flood, the physical limitations of the cultivable area and the immense number of human beings, which, as a result of past history, that area must support. There are those, in the second place, which have their source in defects of economic organisation or in social habits : the absence, for example, of a tolerable system of communications, the miseries inflicted by civil disorder, primitive methods of cultivation, the exploitation of the peasant by dealers and money-lenders, the unsatisfactory character of land tenure in parts of the country, and the tyranny of a tradition which gives an artificial stimulus to the increase of a population already excessive.

These two groups of factors obviously interact; but it is expedient, nevertheless, to distinguish between them. The consideration of methods of ameliorating the conditions of the rural population requires that due account should be given to both. There are the inexorable limits, and the space for manœuvre which the limits allow. It is necessary to eschew both the facile sentimentalism which makes light of the burdens imposed by nature, and the fatalism which ignores the possibilities of scientific knowledge and social art.

(i)

ANALOGOUS PROBLEMS ELSEWHERE

In so far as the disorders of Chinese agriculture belong to the second category, they are acute in degree but not unique in kind. They are one species of a genus which has been widely diffused, and which is characteristic, not of this nation or that, but of a particular phase of economic civilisation. The persistence of an empirical technique based on venerable usage and impervious to science; the meagre output of foodstuffs which that technique produced; the waste of time and labour through the fragmentation of holdings; the profits wrung from the cultivator by middleman, usurer and landlord; the absence of means of communication and the intolerable condition of such as existed; the narrow margin separating the mass of the population from actual starvation and the periodical recurrence of local famines—such phenomena, if exception be made of a few favoured regions, were until recently the commonplaces of western economic life since men first reflected on it. Scientists analysed them; philanthropists deplored them; governments legislated for them; common men confronted their results, sometimes with patient acquiescence, sometimes with violent revolt; in England and France a whole literature arose to expose and correct them. From the Middle Ages to the nineteenth century the social problem of most parts of Europe, in spite of natural advantages of soil and climate, was what in China and India it is to-day. It was the condition, not of the industrial wage-earner, but of the peasant. Its solution, in so far as it has been solved, is a thing of yesterday.

The forces which shifted the scene in the course of the last century need no lengthy explanation. The novelty of the age was the application of science to the productive arts. The effect upon agriculture of the rise of the new technique of manufacture and transport, if indirect, was profound. It turned farming from a subsistence industry into a business enterprise, enabled vast areas of virgin soil to be brought under the plough and their produce to be shipped to distant markets, and, by opening a multitude of new channels of employment, checked the increased pressure on the land, which, given the growth of population, would otherwise have occurred, as effectively as though it had doubled its acreage. But the industrial expansion, which is the most familiar aspect of modern economic history, is one aspect and no more. In Europe it was preceded and accompanied by a movement to modernise agricultural methods and rural organisation, to which the word revolution, if appropriate at all as a description of economic change, is equally applicable.

The innovations introduced were of three principal kinds. They were partly legal and institutional, partly technical and scientific, partly commercial and financial. On ground cleared by the middle of the century of the mediaeval débris—of open-field cultivation, scattered strips, internal barriers to the movement of trade, and the customary tenures that had been the rule on the Continent—a reformed agriculture slowly came to its own. Its marks were the introduction of new crops, the substitution of an intelligent rotation for the wasteful fallow, improved tools and machinery, the use of artificial fertilisers, land drainage and reclamation; its conditions were the progress of scientific knowledge, and the new commercial possibilities created by railways. When, in the 'seventies, the European market was flooded by cheap grain from America and Russia, a third phase began. The English policy of abandoning tillage for pasture was unthinkable on the Continent, with its multitude of small farmers. The first expedient adopted to break the shock was agrarian protection; but more important than the tariff were the measures organised behind it. Cheap transport did much; agricultural research and education ultimately did more. The most significant departure, however, was of a different kind. It was the rapid development of agricultural co-operation.

Agriculture being an industry in which man must wait on nature, the farmer needs resources to finance the interval between his outlay and his return on a scale which, if a small man, he cannot himself supply, while he is bargaining as an individual with sellers and buyers who have larger reserves, and a wider knowledge of markets, than he possesses himself, and who, in addition, are not infrequently organised. In such conditions it is possible for money to be made out of agriculture by money-lenders and middlemen, when the producer himself is on the verge of bankruptcy or starvation. The immemorial hatred of the peasant for the usurer and the engrosser has been the inevitable consequence.

The natural remedy is combined action by farmers to organise for themselves facilities for credit, the marketing of products and the purchasing of supplies. As recently as the middle of the nineteenth century, a rural co-operative movement hardly existed in Europe; but, once established, it developed with surprising rapidity. In Germany, where it dates from the 'sixties, there were in 1922 some 36,000 agricultural societies, including over 19,000 credit societies and over 3,000 dairying societies. In France, where the first society was founded in 1883, there were, by 1914, 6,667 *syndicats* with a membership of over one million. In Denmark, where the first successful society was established in 1882, some 90 per cent of the occupying owners, who farm nearly three-quarters of the cultivated area, were stated in 1918 to be members of co-operative societies—including creameries, bacon factories, butter and cattle export societies, and credit societies, as well as co-operative bakeries, building societies and societies for the generation of electrical power. The effect of the movement, if observers may be trusted, has been, not only to save the farmer part of the middleman's profit and of the interest paid to the money-lender, and to improve the quality of the product by grading and standardisation, but to raise the whole level of social life.

As to the merits and defects of peasant farming in Europe, and the relative importance of the causes through which improvement has taken place, opinions naturally differ. As far as cereals are concerned, it is highly protected; and it is possible that, faced with an intense competition from the machine-farming of Russia and the United States, it will survive only behind an ever-rising tariff. Whatever, however, the future may contain, it would probably be agreed that it has adapted itself to a new situation with a greater degree of success than was anticipated half a century ago, and that the most effective of the agencies which have aided the readjustment have been cheap transport, science and education, and co-operation.

What is not less significant is the lines upon which the modernisation of agriculture has been slowly advancing in certain parts of India. By encouraging farmers not merely to produce for subsistence, but to raise a surplus for the market, and by making possible the easy and expeditious distribution of supplies, railway communications have tended to keep prices throughout the country as a whole more uniform than in the past. The extension of the insurance against drought offered by irrigation, whether by wells, tanks or canals, has contributed to the same result. Primitive methods of cultivation have been slowly yielding to the introduction of improved varieties of crops, seed distribution and the use of better implements. Since 1904, some 67,000 agricultural societies have come into existence, the great majority concerned with the provision of credit; and, while the movement is still in its infancy, in certain provinces it includes from a tenth to a third of the rural population. The division of holdings into scattered plots, which in India, as in the Europe of the past and the China of to-day, offers an obstacle to efficient farming, is in parts of the country being gradually corrected by the progress of consolidation.

Communications, science and education, co-operation in credit and marketing, and the formation, where possible, of compact farms out of dispersed fragments of land, appear everywhere, in short, to be the fundamental conditions of agricultural progress. When methods of promoting it are under consideration, it is upon these matters that attention has commonly been turned.

(ii)

AGRARIAN POLICY

Behind problems of economic organisation stand the brutal facts of nature. Who shall put a hook in the jaws of the Yellow

River or reason the Gobi Desert into blossoming like the rose? But, when the environment is unfavourable, it is not less important, but more important, to exploit to the utmost such opportunities as it offers. Measures which individually appear insignificant produce a cumulative effect, and it is as superficial to despise the day of small things as to hail it with pæans as the dawn of a new era. The plain fact is that, given a reasonable measure of intelligence and public spirit in the quarters responsible for carrying policy into effect, some, at least, of the evils which crush the Chinese peasant to-day are capable of being remedied. The course of wisdom would appear to be to apply such remedies as are available, while recognising that the cure of the disease, if it is curable at all, must be a matter of generations.

That this view is accepted on paper by Chinese governments is suggested by the policy which is understood to have been laid down.[1] As the result of a national congress on agricultural economics and policy held in December, 1929, the Ministry of Agriculture and Mines formulated in January, 1930, a comprehensive programme, which was followed in

[1] The importance of land reform and of the improvement of agriculture has been repeatedly emphasised during the last ten years. Dr. Sun Yat-sen, in his well-known book, spoke of the large share taken by landlords as compared with tenants, declared the goal to be that "each tiller of the soil shall possess his own fields," and emphasised the importance of an increased use of machinery and fertilisers, of a scientific rotation of crops and of the control of pests (*San Min Chu I*, trans. by Frank W. Price, pp. 456–464). The First National Congress of the Kuomintang, in January, 1924, declared that "the Kuomintang stands for the policy that those peasants owning no land should be given land by the State for cultivation," and urged the establishment of rural banks to assist farmers with cheap credit (M. T. Z. Tyau, *Two Years of Nationalist China*, p. 448). The United Council, in October, 1926, drew up a minimum programme of agrarian legislation, which included the reduction of rents by 25 per cent, the establishment of banks in provinces and *hsien* to make loans at 5 per cent to farmers, the prohibition of interest in excess of 20 per cent, prohibition of advance collection of rent, prohibition of sub-letting, and the right of farmers to organise unions (*Chinese Labor Year Book*, Vol. III, pp. 212–213). A Tenant Protection Act was drafted by the Central Kuomintang and promulgated by the Wuhan Government in May, 1927. It laid down that rents paid by tenants were not to exceed 40 per cent of the crop harvested, that tenants should have the right to demand exemption from rent, or its reduction, in case of famine, and that sub-letting be prohibited (*ibid.*, p. 213). For more recent policy see Tyau, *op. cit.*, pp. 177–184. I am indebted to Professor Lamb, of Yenching University, for permission to read part of a study prepared by him of the agrarian policy of the Government.

March, 1930, by the announcement of another adopted in agreement with the Ministries of Communications, Railways and Education, and the Central Committee on Reconstruction. It set out a long series of measures, including the reduction of railway rates on agricultural produce; irrigation and river conservancy; the promotion of co-operative societies for credit and marketing, and of agricultural insurance; the reform of land tenure by the fixing of rents, the establishment of five years as the minimum period for the currency of a lease, and the prohibition of the payment of rent in advance; rural education; the introduction of improved seeds, the prevention of plant diseases and the control of pests; the foundation of a central agricultural experiment station, of a central research institute of agriculture and of model experiment stations in each province; the establishment of factories for the manufacture of agricultural implements and fertilisers; the survey and reclamation of waste land; the creation of a bureau for the reception of immigrants in undeveloped areas, and numerous other items. The lengthy and important Land Law, passed in the course of the same year, conferred on the Land Bureau power to take steps for the consolidation of scattered plots into compact holdings in cases where division appeared economically disadvantageous.[1]

As far, therefore, as programmes are concerned, all the agrarian reforms carried out in other parts of the world in the course of the last century are now part of the official policy of the Government of the Republic. Whether political conditions, administrative machinery and financial resources are such as to enable them to be applied in practice, is a different question, on which a foreigner cannot express an opinion. It may be observed, however, that China is not the only country where life consists of vicious circles and progress of breaking them.

[1] Land Law, Section 1, Chapter 3, Articles 18–20 (*Ministry of Communications Gazette*, July 12, 1930): "If within a particular area the land is divided up in a manner that is economically disadvantageous, the Land Bureau concerned shall have the right to redivide the whole into portions, which shall then be allotted to the original owners." Provision is made for compensating owners the value of whose property has been diminished.

The sensible course is to do first things first, and later to build more extensive reforms on the foundations laid by them.

Nor, as far as this aspect—which is only one aspect—of the problem is concerned, is there serious dispute as to the points at which a beginning should be made. Both on political and economic grounds—though the distinction is unreal—the development of communications is clearly fundamental. On the one hand, the reality of national unity, as distinct from the name, and the absence of internal disorder which such unity implies, are obviously unattainable, as long as it takes almost as much time to travel from the capital to the remoter provinces of China as to go from Nanking to London. On the other hand, the condition of checking the recurrence of famine is that the surplus raised by the farmer for the market should be increased, and that internal trade should be sufficiently developed to enable food supplies to be moved with cheapness and regularity. Chinese methods of agriculture, though more advanced than those of most other countries a century and a half ago, were crystallised in an age when agricultural science was still in its infancy, and could be improved by learning from it. Co-operation for purposes of credit, marketing and the purchase of supplies is the only method yet discovered of protecting small farmers against exploitation by money-lenders and middlemen, and of organising them for mutual assistance and collective action. Conditions of land tenure, if satisfactory in some parts of the country, are in others indefensible. In certain regions the extension of irrigation and the better control of floods are second only in importance to the improvement of transport.

(iii)

COMMUNICATIONS

The present condition of communications in China can be shortly stated. She possesses rather more than 9,500 miles of railway, of which some 4,790 are under the control of the Government, and 3,770 are in the hands of concessionnaires, while the remainder are commercial or industrial lines. The general position can be indicated by saying that the number of persons per mile of railway is roughly 2,200 in the United Kingdom, 1,722 in Germany, 460 in the United States and something over 50,000 in China.

In reality, however, such figures give too favourable a picture of the Chinese situation. Five provinces, including the great and rich territory of Szechwan, with a population almost as large as that of Germany, have no railways at all, while several others have only a few miles. Since there are no through communications from north to south, and the lines in existence are confined to the eastern half of the country, railways have affected but little the economic life of the greater part of China. Approximately three-quarters of the existing lines were built between 1895 and 1915. Partly owing to the European War, partly owing to internal disturbances, development was then checked, and, except in Manchuria, no important extensions have been made in the last ten years. The quality of the system is as deficient as its extent. A general in control of a railway is like a monkey with a watch; and, as a result of civil war, parts of it have been unuseable for commercial purposes for long periods together. Rolling-stock is falling to pieces, and, owing to lack of engineering resources, cannot be put in order. Engines and coaches are detained by rebellious militarists for their private convenience. In some districts the permanent way is out of repair.

The condition of road communications is somewhat more hopeful. Owing to the action of the provincial authorities, the China International Famine Relief Commission, the National Good Roads Council and certain military commanders, who for once did something that was not a curse to their country, considerable progress in building roads has been made in the course of the last decade. Estimates of the mileage vary. According to a valuable report made by the United States Trade Commissioner[1] for the Department of Commerce, in

[1] *Motor Highways in China*, by Viola A. Smith in collaboration with Anselm Chuh (Washington, U.S. Department of Commerce, 1929).

December, 1929, roads suitable for motor traffic then amounted to 34,810 miles, those under construction to 5,055 miles and those projected to 31,099 miles. The greater part of the system has been built since 1920, and some 90 per cent of the roads are said to consist of earth, not of gravel or macadam. Even to-day, there are large areas which are almost untouched. In the province of Kweichow, for example, there were stated, as recently as 1925, to be no roads at all; wheel traffic hardly existed; and the wares required by a population of fourteen million persons were transported on human shoulders.[1] In January, 1929, the Ministry of Railways appointed a National Highway Planning Commission, on the invitation of which a conference attended by the representatives of the provinces was held in the following month. It outlined a programme of development, and urged the construction of 22,518 miles of national highways during the next twenty years, or approximately 1,100 miles a year, to which must be added such roads as may be built by the provincial authorities and voluntary organisations. It may be remarked that, if China were to construct roads continuously at the rate, not of 1,100 miles, but of 10,000 miles a year, she would possess, at the end of 180 years, the same mileage as the United Kingdom, with one-tenth of her population and one-fortieth of her area, possesses to-day.

It is needless to dwell on the economic paralysis which such conditions produce. It was recently found that the cost of transporting 1,400 tons of wheat, for the purpose of famine relief, a distance of 233 miles in Shansi, by carts and pack animals, was 79 cents silver per ton-mile. If moved by tractors and trailers, it would have cost approximately 13 cents; it could have been hauled by rail, had a railway existed, for just under 2 cents. Mass production is obviously impossible unless the output can be marketed, and, in the absence of communications, industrial development is necessarily strangled. The effects upon agriculture and rural life are equally serious. The

---

[1] O. J. Todd, *Engineering and Altruism in China*. A considerable mileage of roads has since then been constructed in Kweichow.

farmer has no incentive to increase his production if he cannot be certain of disposing of it. Owing to the impossibility of choosing his market, he is liable to be bound hand and foot to the local dealers. The specialisation of different regions to different types of farming, with the economies which it offers, is impracticable as long as every district must grow its own supplies of food. The recurrence of local famines is inevitable, since the deficiency of one area cannot be supplemented by the surplus of another.

Motor roads can be built piecemeal, without the heavy capital expenditure required for railways, and are somewhat less liable to be rendered completely useless by civil disturbances. Hence, in the view of good judges, it is by the extension of roads, rather than of railways, that these evils are to be overcome; and, since unemployed labour, in the shape of soldiers, is abundant in China, the extension of roads should present no great difficulty. But what is obviously required to-day is the extension of both, the latter as trunk routes for mass traffic, the former as feeders. The urgency of the need can hardly be overstated. To the layman it appears that the most effective way of aiding China to attain both a larger measure of economic well-being and political stability would be an international loan, with the necessary safeguards against undue interference in her internal affair , for the purpose of enabling her to improve her means of communication.

(iv)

SCIENCE AND EDUCATION

The importance of communications is intellectual and social, as much as economic. They break down rural isolation, circulate ideas as well as commodities, and turn a stream of new interests into stagnant communities. Much is said in China, and very reasonably said, of the necessity of modernising economic methods; but it does not always appear to be fully realised that the need of modernisation, and the possibilities which it opens, are as great in agriculture as in manufacturing industry. Those entitled to an opinion appear to be agreed that, in spite of the proverbial skill of the Chinese farmer, considerable improvements are possible in the technique of farming. Except in Manchuria, the areas adapted to large-scale power farming of the American type do not seem to be extensive. It is a question, not of superseding the traditional system of peasant cultivation, but of grafting on it the improvements made available by the progress of agricultural science.

Those already effected must not be overlooked. New crops, such as peanuts, which have been introduced in the course of the last half-century, have greatly increased the prosperity of certain districts. Careful seed selection has shown that it is possible, in favourable conditions, to double the yield of corn. Fruit farming offers possibilities which some regions have grasped, but which are still ignored by others equally well suited to it, with the result that canned fruits are imported from California which might equally well be grown at home. It is known that, in the case of cotton, tea and silk, in the two latter of which China has lost ground by adhering to antiquated methods, while other countries have advanced, both the output and the quality of the product can be substantially improved. Given the necessary organisation and standards of education, plant and animal diseases can be controlled, and the ravages of pests reduced. Certain parts of China have been under continuous cultivation for a longer period than any other regions in the world, and, if it is incorrect to describe them as suffering from exhaustion, it is probably true, nevertheless, that their yield has been stabilised at a somewhat low minimum. Though artificial fertilisers have not always produced the results expected, the desirability of extending their use is hardly open to question.

The promotion of improved methods of agriculture by research, education and the dissemination of information is in all countries a recent development. In China, where it is more recent than elsewhere, it dates, even on paper, only from the beginning of the present century. The existing agencies are of three main kinds. There is the official machinery of agricultural experiment stations and model farms, maintained by the central Government and certain provincial authorities; the agricultural departments of universities, together with a few schools giving instruction in agriculture; and undertakings established by commercial organisations for testing and grading agricultural products, such as silk and cotton. All have made their contribution; but the introduction of better methods depends not merely on the work of scientific and governmental institutions, but on the degree to which its results are disseminated among those who must apply them in practice. The superficial view that the peasant is too torpid and conservative to adopt improvements offered him is not confirmed by those who know him at first hand. Farmers in China, like farmers everywhere, are, very naturally, sceptical of book knowledge. But the evidence of close observers is that, given ocular demonstration of the practical advantages of, for example, better seeds, they are, in so far as their means allow, quick to take advantage of them.

The weakness of the system, a weakness by no means confined to China, is the divorce which appears frequently to exist between the work of the bodies engaged in research and the practical business of agriculture. If it is largely the inevitable result of the absence of contact between the life of rural China and that of the towns, caused by the deficiency of communications, it is partly also due to the character of the educational system itself. Chinese education, with all its virtues, has some resemblance to a pyramid standing on its point. The schools and colleges giving practical education in agricultural or industrial technology, though some of them are important, are few relatively to the needs of the country. The number of pupils in schools is uncertain; but there were stated in 1931 to be just under 9,000,000 in modern primary schools, and some 780,000 in secondary schools, out of a total population of something over 400,000,000.[1]

The result is that the universities appear sometimes to be

[1] For educational statistics, see below, p. 183.

suspended in the air, that intelligence, which ought to be employed in spreading knowledge of the way to a better existence among the mass of the population, is wasted in a demoralising scramble for openings into careers which are already overcrowded, and that practical life, which in China means overwhelmingly the life of the countryside, is deprived of the stimulus which it might derive from the influence of education. The importance of making increased provision for agricultural research can hardly be exaggerated: improved methods of farming must be tested in a Chinese environment, before they are applied, and tested for a period sufficiently long to enable reliable conclusions to be reached. It is not less essential, however, to grapple with the difficult problem of assuring that those who ought to benefit by the results of research are able to take advantage of them.

What is required, in the first place, is a great increase in the provision for primary education in rural districts, the development of institutions giving practical teaching in agricultural science, and the creation of links between the educational world and the villages. One example of the manner in which such links may be forged is offered by the success achieved in educating farmers in the knowledge of better methods by members of the agricultural departments of certain universities, who live in, or visit, rural areas, and give practical demonstrations of the results to be achieved by applying science to agriculture. Another is to be found in the work done at Ting Hsien by Dr. Y. C. James Yen and his colleagues of the Mass Education Movement. Only those can teach who share in some measure the life of those who are taught. The value of the example set at Ting Hsien does not consist merely in the instruction given or in the practical activities carried on, but in the creation of a community to which the scholar and the farmer both bring their contribution. No one who has attended the classes of agricultural workers conducted there is likely to suppose that the peasant does not appreciate education when opportunities for it are offered to him. The tragedy is that the opportunities which exist at present are so few.

(v)

CO-OPERATION[1]

The extension of education is the foundation of all other necessary improvements. It is the most certain way of enabling the rural population to help itself. Its results should be not merely an improvement in methods of farming, but the introduction of a better system of credit and marketing, in the absence of which the producer is at the mercy of the money-lender and the dealer.

Simple forms of co-operation, in the shape of mutual benefit and loan societies, have existed from time immemorial among Chinese peasants. The significant development in the last ten years has been the growth of an agricultural co-operative movement of a modern type on a permanent basis. Its initiation was due partly to the work of the China International Famine Relief Commission, partly to the Agricultural College of the University of Nanking. A committee on credit and economic improvement had been appointed by the Commission in May, 1922. The first society to be founded appears to have been the Feng Ren Co-operative Credit Society, consisting principally of vegetable growers, which was organised by the University of Nanking, with the aid of a grant from the Commission in September, 1923. A few months later, rules for co-operative societies were drawn up; at the beginning of 1924 three societies were recognised; and the first loan in aid of co-operation was made by the Commission in February, 1924. The progress made by the movement since that date is mainly due to the advice and financial assistance that the Commission has given.

[1] Paul C. Hsu, *Rural Co-operation in China* (Institute of Pacific Relations, Honolulu, 1929); Chunjen C. C. Chen, *Agricultural Co-operative Movement in China* (*China Critic*, July 4 and 11, 1929); China International Famine Relief Commission, *Annual Report*, 1929, and *Herr Raiffeisen among Chinese Farmers*, 1930; *Statistics of the Rural Credit Co-operative Societies in Chekiang Province, Investigated by the Bureau of Reconstruction of Chekiang Province*, January, 1930 (Chinese); J. B. Tayler, *Denmark and Rural China* (*Chinese Social and Political Science Review*, Vol. XII, No.1, January, 1928).

The position at the end of 1929, as far as societies within the purview of the Commission were concerned, was that 816 societies, with 21,934 members, had been established, of which 244 were found on investigation to be satisfactorily organised, and had accordingly been recognised, while 572 had not yet received recognition. The federalism everywhere characteristic of co-operation had begun to develop, and local unions had been formed. With two exceptions, all the societies connected with the Commission were in a single province, that of Hopei, but independent movements are now growing up in other parts of the country. In 1927 the Government of Kiangsu, and in 1928 that of Chekiang, began to interest themselves in the promotion of co-operation among farmers. Some hundreds of societies were stated in 1929 to exist in those provinces,[1] and both they and certain others had established rural banks for the assistance of agriculture. Finally, in March 1930, the Government gave its endorsement to the movement. The agricultural programme then adopted stated that the encouragement of agricultural co-operation was part of its policy, urged provincial authorities to establish schools for training co-operative leaders, and laid down that co-operative societies should be registered with the Government. Such declarations, whatever their effect in practice, presumably mean that the movement has become sufficiently important for politicians to be aware of its existence.

No adequate materials for estimating the extent of agricultural co-operation in China are at present available. It is probable, however, that the total number of societies does not exceed, at most, 1,500, or the total membership 100,000. In comparison with the number of persons engaged in agriculture, the movement is obviously insignificant. But it is not more insignificant than it was in 1850 in those European countries where to-day it is a power, and the more important fact is that, ten years ago, there was in China no movement at all.

[1] In January, 1930, there were in Chekiang 143 rural credit societies in 15 *hsiens*, with an individual membership ranging from 11 to 560, and an aggregate membership of 4,524 (Report of Bureau of Reconstruction of Chekiang Province, *Statistics of Rural Credit Co-operative Societies*, January, 1930).

To discount the value of co-operation on the ground that the groups most directly benefited by it are likely to be those which are furthest removed from privation, if a plausible criticism, is, on a long view, a superficial one. Ambulance work is necessary and beneficial, but it is not a substitute for a healthy regimen. To raise the mass, one must find a leverage. The measures which ultimately produce the largest results are not those which take as their objective the immediate relief of actual destitution, indispensable though that is, but those which create the habits and institutions that, in time, may prevent destitution from occurring.

Judged from that angle, the advantage offered by a vigorous co-operative movement can hardly be exaggerated; and a vigorous movement implies, it must be remembered, not merely financial assistance, which, when unaccompanied by other measures, is liable to be abused, but propaganda, organisation, supervision and, above all, education. It is needless to dwell on the vital importance of improving farming technique, which has very properly claimed a large share of the attention devoted to agricultural questions in China. Agriculture is not only, however, a productive art; it is also a difficult business enterprise, with financial and commercial problems of its own. In so far as it fails to solve them—in so far as the peasant is loaded with exorbitant interest charges and crippled by a wasteful and ineffective system of distribution—it may be conducted with admirable skill as a productive industry, but those engaged in it lose as business men what they make as farmers. In so far as a rational organisation is created for dealing with questions of credit, marketing, supplies and insurance, it not only protects the producer against exploitation, but provides, in addition, a lever which can be used to raise the general level of productive efficiency. "Better business, better farming, better living," which has been the motto of agricultural co-operation in western countries, sets the essential issues in the proper order. The foundation on which other indispensable improvements are most easily and securely built is machinery through which credit can be secured on reason-

able terms, and orderly marketing substituted for the alter-
nating periods of glut and scarcity which make farming a
gamble, and a gamble with dice heavily loaded against the
farmer.

Agricultural co-operation is concerned with several different
needs, and one type of co-operation naturally helps another.
A small number of Chinese societies have undertaken with
success the marketing of produce and the purchase of supplies.
But in China, as in Germany, the movement began with the
object of making credit available for agriculture at equitable
rates, and hitherto it has been almost wholly concerned with
that side of the farmer's business. The records of the China
International Famine Relief Commission show that between
one-third and one-half of the advances made are under twenty
dollars, and that, together with the repayment of old debts, the
principal object for which they are obtained are the purchase
of grain, seed, stock, food for animals, and implements.[1]
It is not the least of the evils of the present situation that,
where capital could be used to the greatest general advantage,
it hardly exists, and, where it exists, it cannot be used, or
used to good purpose. Rural China is crying out for it, and,
instead of being employed to finance agricultural improvement, it is diverted to speculation in land values in Shanghai.
Interest rates as high as those charged to Chinese peasants
are a crushing tax on agricultural progress; and, since the
heaviest millstone round the neck of the Chinese farmer
is usury, it is natural that co-operative societies should have
been primarily concerned with its removal. But the inefficiency
of the marketing system, and the opportunities which it
offers to the dealer to exploit the producer, are a hardly
less serious evil. The appropriate remedy, and, as experience proves, an effective remedy, is the co-operative selling
of agricultural produce, which is practised to-day in all
peasant countries of the West, and the most brilliant·example
of which has been given by Denmark.

Once co-operation is firmly established, it can be extended

[1] See above, p. 53, note 3.

from agriculture to the crafts carried on in connection with it. In view of the long periods of enforced idleness to which the farmer is exposed—he is said, in parts of China, not to be employed in agriculture for more than a hundred days in the year—by-employments which supplement his income ought obviously to be encouraged. In the majority of European countries, and particularly in those with large peasant populations, rural industries carried on in the cottages of the workers still play a more important part than is commonly realised. In China, the impression of a superficial observer is that hardly a district is without one or more of them. The dexterity, ingenuity, resourcefulness and, above all, sense of beauty of her common people are a social and economic asset of inestimable value. The course of wisdom, it may be suggested, is to build upon them. It is to retain, where possible, as Professor Tayler[1] urges, the small productive units which are the traditional form of industrial organisation in China, but to secure for them the advantages of large-scale methods in finance and commerce, by taking steps to promote the formation of co-operative societies for credit, marketing and the purchase of raw materials.

Nor are the provision of cheap credit and the elimination of superfluous distributive charges the only benefits which co-operation confers. Its educative influence is more fundamental and far-reaching than the immediate financial and commercial advantages accruing from it. By organising the rural population, it creates a temper of mutual confidence, a consciousness of common needs, and a habit of collective action. In time, it may be hoped, it will enable the peasants in China, as in other countries, to carry their proper weight in the public affairs which affect them, and in the conduct of which they appear to-day to be sacrificed without compunction. There is no movement on which a group of men who desire to improve the life of the farmer can engage with greater certainty of producing permanent results.

[1] J. B. Tayler, *A Policy for Small-Scale Industry* (National Christian Council, Shanghai, 1931).

(vi)

LAND TENURE

While a beginning has been made with agricultural co-operation, the thorny question of land tenure remains almost untouched. If in the north, where occupying ownership preponderates, it is of secondary importance, in parts of southern and central China it is serious. Grievances have been exploited, no doubt, for political purposes; but to ascribe the bitter agrarian struggles which have occurred in parts of the country merely to the effects of propaganda is naïve in the extreme. Such phenomena are common in all countries where the peasant pays a considerable part of his income to an absentee owner. In China, they are, if anything, more inevitable than elsewhere. The fact is that holdings of the size which is common will not provide a living both for the cultivator and the landlord, unless the latter pays his way by putting as much into the business of agriculture as he takes out of it, which he sometimes does, but sometimes does not. When he is a mere incubus, not a partner in the concern, it is inevitable that the peasants in China, as everywhere else, should resent his exactions.

The problem has two aspects, which are often confused. It consists partly in the exploitation of the tenant by rack-renting, which, when no service is performed by the landlord, is doubly exasperating; partly in the existence, side by side with the tiny holdings of the majority of peasants, of large blocks of land in the occupation of individuals, which, though exceptional in China, are found in certain districts, and which are resented as diminishing the area available for cultivation by their poorer neighbours. Neither condition, of course, is peculiar to China. The grievances arising from them both form a long and tragic chapter in the social history of Europe, a chapter which has been closed only in the recent past.

When, towards the end of the eighteenth century, and at intervals throughout the nineteenth, agrarian reform received serious attention in Europe, the policies adopted followed two main paths, which, though often crossing, aimed at different objectives. On the one hand, steps were taken to turn tenants into owners, and thus to relieve the cultivator of the payments in money or in kind previously made to a landlord. On the other hand, measures were applied to augment the size of peasant holdings by adding to them land taken from large properties. An illustration of the first is to be found in the expropriation of feudal landowners in France between 1789 and 1793, the encouragement given to the Danish peasants to redeem their rents and labour services with the aid of state credit, and the arrangement, less favourable to the tenants, under which, in Prussia, they were enabled to acquire full ownership of part of their buildings, in return for the cession of the remainder to their landlords. The second is illustrated by the land settlement, *Innere Kolonisation*, or small holdings policy, pursued in Denmark, Germany and, though on an insignificant scale, in England, which has had as its purpose to increase the size or number of small farms with land compulsorily acquired from large estates.

In China, with its immense agricultural population, the land question is so obviously fundamental that it has naturally attracted the attention of all who are concerned with the economic and political progress of the nation.[1] Programmes of reform adopted by the Kuomintang have included, since 1924, measures for making land available for peasants, and the reduction of rents by 25 per cent. The elaborate policy of agricultural development and reconstruction agreed upon by the Ministries concerned in March, 1930, dealt with the subject of land tenure in greater detail. It does not appear to have proposed measures, other than the reclamation of waste land, for increasing the number of occupying owners; but it is stated to have laid down that the policy of the Government was to make a survey of the present system of tenancy in all localities, to fix rent on all agricultural lands, to prescribe a minimum period of five years as the term for which land should be let,

---

[1] See above, pp. 83–84.

to forbid the payment of rent in advance, the collection of taxes by landlords, and other forms of extortion, and to establish conciliation and arbitration committees for the settlement of disputes between landlords and tenants. Proposals put forward from the left in the course of the same year urged that all farmers should be enabled to own their own farms, and that, presumably as a step in that direction—though the connection is not clear—a maximum limit should be fixed by law to the size of holdings.   148572

When land is as scarce, and population as dense, as in parts of China they are to-day, there is much to be said for the policy of increasing the size of the smaller holdings by limiting the size of the larger. As far as Manchuria and certain other exceptional regions are concerned, the policy of breaking up large estates, and making the land obtained available for small farmers, is capable of application, and should be applied. But, apart from these special cases, its possibilities are narrow. Though there are some large properties, the majority of them are already let out in small holdings worked by peasants, so that the area available for redistribution is in most regions exiguous. In such conditions, the only method of effecting any general increase in the acreage of holdings would appear to be to find alternative employment for part of the population seeking a living from the land.

The problem of protecting tenants against exploitation stands on a different footing. Its solution is urgent and, given the necessary machinery, practicable; the only question is that, not of principle, but of procedure. The simplest and most effective course, for which there are many precedents in the history of other countries, is to use public credit to make it easy for tenants to become owners, and at the same time to exercise compulsion on landlords to sell. Under existing conditions, the practical difficulty is, of course, the financial one. The policy of a general reduction of rents by 25 per cent, which has been proposed in certain quarters, has, apart from the immediate benefit to tenants, the further advantage of encouraging landlords to part with their property—a result, it is stated, already produced in one district that has applied it —and of ensuring that, when they sell, an inflated price will not be paid for the land. The objection to it is that the relations of landlords and tenants are of extreme diversity, with the result that rent means different things in different places, and that merely to diminish it by one quarter, without regard to local circumstances and without readjustments to meet them, would frequently create as many problems as it solved.

The very variety of customs, which differ widely from place to place in the rights which they accord to landlord and tenant, itself offers, indeed, a possible basis for a policy. An alternative course to a flat reduction of rents would be, in fact, to ascertain the best custom obtaining, and to make it of general application, with the necessary local variations to suit local conditions. It might be suggested, for example, that the reasonable custom under which, in parts of the country, the tenant has security while he pays his rent, which the landlord cannot raise, and can freely sell, mortgage and bequeath his rights in the land, should be taken as a model, and tenures elsewhere, so far as circumstances allowed, assimilated to it. Were that course adopted, the most serious grievances of tenants would be removed; and, though the value of the land-lord's interest would in certain areas be diminished, it could hardly be said that they possessed, as a class, any strong ground for complaint. Those whose claims are most exorbitant would merely be compelled to fall into line with their more reasonable and less privileged neighbours.

The proposal to fix rents by public action, which is contained in the programme adopted in the spring of 1930, presumably implies the establishment of fair-rent courts, for the purpose of revising rents downwards and of dealing with other grievances of tenants. As far as is known, machinery for carrying it out still remains to be created. The policy, however, is a familiar one, and, though attended by practical difficulties, is not in itself unreasonable. A somewhat similar suggestion has been made by Professor Buck. As a result of his investigations of agricultural conditions in north and east-central China, he concludes that rents are excessive. Family earnings per adult male worker are 20 per cent less, he points out, in the case of tenants than in that of owners; while, if the division of receipts in proportion to the respective contributions of farmer and landlord be taken as the criterion of a fair rent, the share taken by the former is at present too small. He accordingly proposes that machinery should be set up to effect a readjustment, district by district, in accordance with the different conditions of different localities.

Until more experience is available, however, than exists to-day, the discussion of such measures is necessarily remote from reality. The important thing is not the further enunciation of laudable principles, but that a beginning should be made with their practical application, on however humble a scale, in some specific area. If any government takes up seriously the question of land reform, which no government yet has, it must attack it by stages, and create permanent machinery for the purpose. It must select one or more districts where the problem is particularly acute, and appoint a standing Commission to prepare and carry out a scheme appropriate to the special needs of the areas in question. The Commission should have the duty of fixing rents and revising contracts between landlords and tenants, of requiring the former to surrender land to which no title can be shown, and of carrying through a policy of compulsory land purchase, the cost being divided between the tenant and the state. The same machinery should be used to deal with the analogous question of the consolidation of holdings. The problem is one of extreme complexity, affecting, in greater or less degree, several million farmers. Its settlement in Europe was a matter of centuries, and in India, in spite of recent progress, it has not more than begun. If it is to be solved in China, it will be solved piecemeal. It is only when some particular region has shown the possibility of a more rational system, that the precedent set is likely to be followed.

(vii)

DROUGHT AND FLOOD

Communications, better methods of farming, education, co-operation, and the improvement of the condition of the tenant farmer, are matters which concern, though in different degrees, all parts of China. There are certain evils, however, the incidence of which is felt with particular weight by particular regions. The most serious of them are drought and flood. The districts affected have some resemblance to the black spots created by trade depression in other parts of the world. The difference is that the latter suffer from distress, and the former from starvation.

The prevention of famine is partly a matter of transport. It may occur, at present, even when there is a surplus of food within a few hundred miles of the area threatened with it. It depends partly, however, on the possibility of mitigating the local causes which produce it. The attempt to control the environment by irrigation and flood prevention is the most venerable part of Chinese agricultural policy. The question now is how far these measures can be extended with the aid of modern engineering resources. The issues involved are technical, and a lay view of them is worthless. Expert opinion appears to incline to the conclusion that it is possible, at any rate, substantially to reduce the area threatened by disaster. While the rainfall is obviously a limiting factor, drought occurs at present in regions where adequate supplies of water exist, but where there are no efficient means of making it available for agriculture; while it is stated that plans have been prepared which, if carried into effect, would make almost immune to floods districts which hitherto have periodically suffered from them. The well-known work of the China International Famine Relief Commission supplies an illustration of the possibilities of a preventive policy. In addition to the building of roads, large numbers of wells have been dug for the purpose of irrigating farm lands; canals have been constructed, one of which, when completed, will enable, it is estimated, a population of a million and a quarter to carry on farming with reasonable security; flood-prevention works have been carried out with the result of making it possible to grow crops to the value of $10,000,000 on an area where agriculture was formerly precarious.[1] Apart from natural difficulties, the principal obstacles to the extension of such a policy are lack of financial resources, the deficiency of a skilled personnel, and civil war. In so far as the latter are removed, it is held by good judges that the former can, to some considerable extent, be overcome.

(viii)

POPULATION, MIGRATION AND THE DEVELOPMENT OF INDUSTRY

Whether, if they were overcome, a substantial advance in the standard of life of the rural population would take place, is another question. Granted, it may be urged, the desirability of modernising methods of agriculture, improving its financial and commercial organisation, diffusing education, extending communications, reforming the tenure of land where reform is needed, and checking the occurrence of drought and flood, is much, after all, to be expected from such measures? The larger problems are of a kind with which these and similar well-intentioned reforms do not begin to cope. The fundamental fact, it is urged, is of a terrible simplicity. It is that the population of China is too large to be supported by existing resources. While, in China as a whole, its mean density is low compared with that of most western countries, in certain areas it is appalling. Whole provinces, as large as European states, may properly be described as congested districts. The struggle of a swarm of human beings for a bare physical existence is an ever-present reality. All the phenomena of rural distress—minute holdings, tiny incomes, female infanticide, starvation—are the

[1] O. J. Todd, *Engineering and Altruism in China*; and China International Famine Relief Commission, *Annual Report*, 1929.

unavoidable result of it. The catastrophes which shock the West are merely the sensational revelations of a process of readjustment which is continuous and inevitable. They are the occasions, so to say, on which nature shows her hand. Famine is the economic, civil war the political, expression of the pressure of population on the means of subsistence.

It is true that the population attempting to live by agriculture is in China excessive; the practical proof is that so many persons die. It is true that this population is badly distributed in relation to present resources, with the result that the chances of life are much smaller in some regions than in others. It is true that Chinese habit and doctrine put a premium on the growth of population, which appears to western eyes unnatural and artificial. Sentiment, hallowed by immemorial tradition, makes it a duty to leave sons, and the communism of the patriarchal family dissociates the production of children from responsibility for their maintenance. Hence prudential restraints act with less force than elsewhere; and population, instead of being checked by the gradual tightening of economic pressure on individuals, plunges blindly forward, till whole communities go over the precipice. Apart from the improvement of methods of agriculture, the principal expedients adopted elsewhere, though extremely various, may be reduced to three—migration, the development of alternative sources of livelihood, and the deliberate limitation of the size of families. The question is how far any or all of them are applicable to China, and what, if applied, their effect would be.

Emigration from China has taken place for many centuries, but the number of Chinese now living abroad is not large. It is put by good authorities at no more than 6,000,000 to 7,000,000. Migration within China has been hampered in the past by the absence of means of communication, political disorder, the pious affection which binds the peasant to the graves of his ancestors, the fact that Chinese farming is somewhat closely connected with the market and does not readily move in advance of it, and the policy of the Tsing dynasty in closing Manchuria to colonisation from the south.

Comparisons of the total area of the country with its cultivated acreage are liable to be misleading; large parts of it are too dry, too cold or too rough for successful agriculture. Certain provinces of China proper, if adequately equipped with communications, would probably carry a larger population; but scientific opinion does not seem at present to support the suggestion that the cultivated area could be greatly increased by extensive machine-farming. The principal regions available for colonisation are the north-east and north-west. The possibilities of the north-west are still largely unknown; but much of it is mountainous; the growing season is short; and the isohyets bend south towards the west, so that the average rainfall is said not to exceed 8 to 10 inches, and probably only the eastern fringe is fit for settlement. Its present political conditions are not favourable to colonisation; the insecurity of life in Inner Mongolia is such, indeed, that many farmers with land there do not spend the year on their holdings, but abandon them as soon as the harvest is sold, rather than stay and be robbed. The north-east has been the scene in the last ten years of one of the greatest migrations in the history of the world.

The average immigration into Manchuria for the four years from 1923 to 1926 is put at 514,070. Then in 1927, a year of famine, it bounded up, reaching the astonishing figure of 1,178,254, and averaging for the three years 1927–29, 1,021,005. It is significant that, whereas, seven years ago, the movement was still largely seasonal, workers arriving in spring and leaving in autumn, it has since then increasingly tended to be migration with a view to permanent settlement, and that the proportion of women taking part in it has increased. On the other hand, apart from seasonal migration, there is a large return flow from Manchuria, through failure to find a home there or disillusionment with its conditions, which are often, if accounts may be trusted, of almost incredible severity. In 1927, 67 per cent of the immigrants remained as colonists in Manchuria, in 1928, 58 per cent, and in 1929, 41 per cent. Figures for 1930 are not yet available, but it is probable that they will show a further decline. The net immigration—arrivals less returns—for the seven years 1923–29 is estimated to have amounted to 2,441,868.[1]

Manchuria has an area of approximately 380,000 square miles, about four and a half times that of Great Britain. The present population is said to be just over 30,000,000, of whom roughly one-half, some 14,500,000, are found in Liaoning, about 9,000,000 in Kirin, and just over 5,000,000, or something under a sixth, in the northern province of Heilungkiang. The last has an area of 211,000 square miles, or over 20 per cent more than both the others together. Its density of population was put in 1926 at 24 per square mile; and, out of a cultivable area put at 20,500,000 acres, just over one-third, some 7,200,000 acres, was stated to be cultivated. It is in the northern parts of Kirin and Heilungkiang that the most important developments are to be expected. Mr. Yashnoff, one of the principal authorities on the subject, estimates that the cultivated land and population of northern Manchuria might possibly be trebled, and that this might conceivably take place in the next forty years. On the other hand, granted that the territory is capable of carrying, even without any considerable measure of industrialisation, a population of 25,000,000 to 40,000,000, there are, as Dr. Young points out, a number of other factors to be taken into account.[2] The lack of communications, the necessity of adapting Chinese methods of agriculture to a shorter growing season, the insecurity of life and property, are among them.

The obstacles are formidable, but they are not much more grave than those encountered in the past by colonists in some other parts of the world. It is extraordinary that, within a few

[1] Figures from *Report on Progress in Manchuria, 1907–28* (South Manchuria Railway Company, Dairen, 1929). Other estimates are somewhat lower. According to figures compiled in March, 1931, arrivals during 1930 were about 500,000 and departures about 300,000.

[2] For the whole subject see C. Walter Young, *Chinese Colonisation in Manchuria* (*Problems of the Pacific*, 1929, p. 460) and the digest of Mr. E. E. Yashnoff's book, *Chinese Agriculture in Northern Manchuria* (Harbin, 1926), made for the Institute of Pacific Relations. More recently, the admirable book of Mr. Owen Lattimore, *Manchuria, Cradle of Conflict*, has thrown a flood of new light on the whole subject.

days' journey of Hopei and Shantung, in parts of which population is over 2,000 to the square mile, and famine is recurrent, great areas of rich land should be available for settlers, and that only within the last ten years should mass migration on a grand scale have begun. The population and culture of Manchuria are overwhelmingly Chinese. Movement into it has taken place under the influence of extremely diverse motives, and has assumed many different forms. It is probably true to say, however, that the migration most characteristic of the last decade has been a flight of refugees, whose hearts remained in China, rather than an advance of pioneers courting the opportunities and dangers of virgin territory. It has resembled in its procedure the squeezing of water from a sponge. Unhappy peasants have sometimes been packed into ships like cattle, except that cattle would be supplied with food and water, to be landed, without resources, in a country where the winter lasts for six months; where they must somehow acquire land, tools and seed, and raise one year's crop on pain of starvation; where some of them, being unable to afford the price of a railway ticket, must tramp some hundreds of miles to their destination; and where, when they arrive, they are liable to be robbed by one set of bandits who are called by that name, and another set masquerading as landlords and officials. It is not surprising that migration has proceeded, not regularly, but by sudden spurts, under the pressure of famine, that the mortality among settlers is high, and that the backward ebb, with all the waste and misery which it involves, is enormous. What is obviously required is the establishment of more efficient machinery for selecting immigrants, with due consideration both to individual fitness and to local overpopulation, for aiding their movement, for assisting them on their arrival, as is done in other countries, with information and equipment, and for protecting them against robbery and murder. The agricultural programme of the Government includes measures for aiding migration. It is to be hoped that means will be found for carrying them into effect.

Migration is not a solution, of course, of the problem of

over-population. Under existing conditions, the most it can do—if, indeed, it can do that—is slightly to relax the strain of abnormal local pressure, and accord a brief breathing space. The development of manufacturing and extractive industries, using machinery and power, is often advanced as a more fundamental remedy. In Europe it has been the principal reason why a population of some 500,000,000 persons can be supported to-day at a higher standard of life than that of the 180,000,000 who existed in 1800. The effects of industrialisation, it is urged, as distinct from modernisation—which is as applicable to agriculture as to manufacturing industry—are partly direct, partly indirect. On the one hand, by increasing the output of wealth per head, it makes possible a higher income for the worker engaged in the new industries than was offered by agriculture, and adds to the resources at the disposal of the state. On the other hand, by creating new employments, it slows down the rate of growth of the agricultural population, even if it does not diminish its absolute number; prevents an increase of pressure on the land, with the disastrous sub-division of holdings which such pressure produces; creates new and more remunerative markets for the farmer; makes accessible to him cheap transport, tools and fertilisers; and thus facilitates an improvement in agriculture and an increase in its product. But, before considering the possibilities of industrialisation, it will be convenient to glance briefly at the facts of industry.

CHAPTER V

THE OLD INDUSTRIAL ORDER AND THE NEW

Endowed with large areas of fertile soil, valuable raw materials, and a high tradition of tests and skill, China has long possessed important manufacturing industries. Till the rise of machine production a century and a half ago, her technique was identical in character with that of the West, and, in quality, not infrequently superior to it. "Our Celestial Empire possesses all things in prolific abundance, and lacks no product within its own borders; there is therefore no need to import the manufactures of outside barbarians"[1]—the oft-quoted reply in which her Government rebuffed in 1793 the British proposal for closer trade relations, if politically naïve, had more economic justification than the West supposed. It was given at a moment when the greater number of British industries were still only emerging from much the same phase of development as those of China, and when certain among them had been striving for a century to master the lessons taught by Chinese craftsmanship.

(i)

THE LEGACY OF THE PAST

During the three generations in which the Industrial Revolution was travelling round the world, that phase survived in China with but little modification. As far as the greater part of the country is concerned, it survives to-day, though with increasing erosion. No occupational census has been taken in China. Figures,[2] of doubtful reliability, are available for cer-

[1] See the Imperial Mandate of Ch'ien Lung to George III on the occasion of Lord Macartney's mission in 1793, quoted in E. Backhouse and J. O. P. Bland, *Annals of the Court of Peking* (1914), p. 326.

[2] Occupational censuses have been taken for the provinces of Kiangsu (1919) and Shansi (1923), for Kwangtung Territory (1924), and for the cities of Nanking (1925), Tsingtao (1926), and Canton (1928). See *The Chinese Labor Year Book*, 1928, Vol. I, pp. 2–5, and *Nankai Weekly Statistical Service*, Vol. IV, No. 2, January 12, 1931.

tain provinces and cities in particular years, but both the numbers engaged in different industries, and the size of the urban[1] population, are a matter of conjecture. Factory industry, based on power and machinery, has been advancing for more than thirty years in certain limited areas. Its record, with some honourable exceptions, has not been good, and the question of the conditions under which it is to develop is one of the vital problems confronting China. The standards obtaining in factory employment are necessarily influenced, however, by those prevailing outside it, and the greater part of the country stands at present on a different plane of economic civilisation.

Here and there, even in the interior, where roads, rivers or railways make a highway for change, a cluster of chimneys towers over fields worn by the patient routine of two thousand years. But the system that they represent, which in western Europe is the rule, is in China the exception. In technique and organisation the major part of her industry belongs either to the pre-capitalist era or to the first infancy of capitalism. Its characteristics are not power-driven machinery, joint-stock finance and a hierarchy of economic authority, but primitive tools, handicraft methods, and minute investments of capital by merchants or small masters controlling a multiplicity of tiny undertakings. European analogies with which to compare

---

[1] The number of places described as towns in the Post Office Statistics of 1920 was 1,910. It was estimated by the Customs authorities in 1927 that the population of 15 cities with over 200,000 inhabitants was 8,662,300. According to the *China Year Book*, 1926, there were 36 cities with over 1,000,000 inhabitants each. For a discussion of the subject, see Boris P. Torgasheff, *Town Population in China* (*The China Critic*, April 3, 1930). Using a large number of different sources, Mr. Torgasheff has calculated that the population of 112 cities, with over 100,000 inhabitants, was, in 1930, 30,830,400; of 178 cities, with 50,000 to 100,000, 11,556,400; and of 177 cities, with 25,000 to 50,000 inhabitants, 8,064,700; making a total of 50,451,500 inhabitants for 467 cities. When account is taken of the remaining 1,443 towns on the official list, and of those which should probably be included in it, but are not, the total town population of China should be put, he suggests, at not far short of 100,000,000. There is some reason for thinking that the estimate is too high, and that a total of 75,000,000 would be nearer the truth. In that case the urban population of China may possibly form between 16 and 20 per cent of her total population. It must be remembered, however, that many town-dwellers are engaged in agriculture.

it must be sought, not in the twentieth century, but from the fourteenth to the early nineteenth.

These features are found even in those branches of enterprise which, in the West, are the peculiar stronghold of large-scale industry. Between one-third and one-half of the output of coal, and one-fifth of that of iron ore, have been estimated to be produced by small native mines employing a few score of workers apiece and almost destitute of machinery.[1] The Chinese iron industry has the longest continuous history in the world, and had mastered the art of making cast-iron some fifteen hundred years before that of Europe; but nearly one-half of the pig-iron produced is made in charcoal furnaces, with bellows worked by hand or water power. Cotton-spinning is the industry which first entered the factory, and in which factory production has proceeded furthest; but some of the spinning and, as in the England of the early nineteenth century, the greater part of the weaving, still continues to be done either at home or in small workshops. Side by side with machine production and large-scale organisation in these, and perhaps a dozen other, branches of production, are some hundreds of industries to which western methods have hardly begun to be applied. The crafts of the worker in metal, whether iron, copper, tin or silver; of the potter and tile-maker, of the builder, carpenter, furniture-maker, painter, shoe-maker, hat-maker, tailor, tanner, wood-carver, lacquer-maker, of silk reeling and weaving, woollen-weaving, tapestry-making, rope-making, as well as the innumerable trades concerned with the production of household requirements, ornaments, jewellery, and artistic products, though often indirectly affected by changing commercial and financial methods, are still much what they were five centuries ago.

The attempts of historians to classify stages of industrial development have rarely been felicitous. The reality is too fluid to be compressed within neat boundaries of genus and species. Types overlap and melt into each other; identity of

---

[1] *Mining Labor in China*, by Boris Torgasheff (*Chinese Economic Journal*, Vol. VI, No. 4, April, 1930).

form conceals difference of fact. Hans Sachs turns out, on closer examination, to be, not the independent master-craftsman of the mediaeval legend, but a sub-contractor, at once sweated and sweating, to a capitalist merchant. The merchant in one capacity is a factory-owner in another. The factory, so far from resembling a modern spinning mill or engineering works, may be in fact, as in China till recently it was in law, a primitive workshop, unequipped with machinery or power, housing less than two score workers. All alike may stand in a dozen different relations to the financier, the purveyor of raw materials and the market. If some two to three thousand great concerns be for the moment ignored, what exists in China is what existed in Europe before the rise of the great industry, and still survives, if precariously, in its crannies and back-waters. It is less an organised industrial system than a labyrinth or spider's web of small undertakings, each working under conditions peculiar to itself, and isolated by difficulties of communication from all but those in its immediate neighbourhood.

Two threads in the fabric, which in Europe have slipped, are still important in China. The family, consisting, as it does, not merely of parents and children, but of a group embracing three or four generations and their collaterals living together, retains an economic significance which it has long lost in the West. It acts on occasion as an industrial unit, which supplies its own needs and produces for the market. When, twenty years ago, a Chinese economist[1] investigated conditions in his native district of Ningpo, he estimated that 40 per cent of the families cultivated cotton, which they cleaned, prepared, spun and wove in their own homes. Though family work has declined, it still survives, especially in rural districts. It is not uncommon for peasants not only to grow their own food, but to build their own cottages, to produce the material required for their clothes, to card and spin the cotton or wool, and to weave the cloth. There are, again, a multitude of

[1] Nyok-Ching Tsur, *Die Gewerblichen Betriebsformen der Stadt Ningpo in China*, Tübingen, 1909, pp. 17–35.

isolated craftsmen who work for customers, sometimes on the premises of the latter and with materials supplied by them. They make their rounds, like tinkers or knife-grinders in the West, from dawn to dusk, and the streets of cities resound with their cries.

The characteristic organisation of industry is, however, different, though the family often remains the nucleus round which it is built. It takes the form partly of handicrafts carried on in the shops of small masters, partly of work done on commission for merchants, who distribute raw materials, supply credit and market the produce. In theory distinguished by the fact that, in the first case, the master is an independent producer dealing direct with the market, and, in the second, a contractor employed by a wholesaler, in practice the two types overlap. The merchant may find it convenient at one time to buy the wares produced in a small master's shop, and at another to employ him on a commission basis. The small master may work to the order of the merchant when business is brisk, and struggle on by himself in times of depression.

Some form of what the English Commissions of the early nineteenth century, who saw it in its ruin, called the small-master system is universal in China, both in the cities and, still more, in the villages and country towns. In Tayinchen, in the south of Hopei, to give one example, the tanning of the skins collected from the neighbouring farmers is carried on in workshops, the smallest of which are staffed by the members of a single family and some two-fifths by less than 10 workmen, while a few considerable firms employ a personnel of as many as 100, and the majority about 20 to 25, the finished article being sold to dealers from the commercial centres. In the potting industry of P'eng Cheng, in the same province, some 81 potteries own 211 kilns for the manufacture of bowls, with 20 to 30 workmen apiece. In the fur and leather industry of Swanhwa, the Bureau of Economic Information reported in 1925 the existence of about 60 shops, the six largest of which employed over 100 men each, and the majority between 40 and 80. In the famous porcelain industry of Kingtchen, which has profoundly influenced the art of the western potter, the system of small independent masters obtains.[1]

But examples are endless. The traveller who explores the streets of any Chinese town passes between rows of houses open to the streets, at once workshops and homes, in which small groups of artisans are hammering metal, fashioning wood, or making clothing and shoes, side by side with their employers, whose meals they share, and with whom, when apprentices, they normally lodge. In the more pretentious establishments, and more delicate crafts, like fan-making and lantern-making, the front serves as a shop where wares are displayed; the rooms and courts behind it are the workshops where materials are stored, work is carried on from dawn to dusk, and food is prepared. There is little sub-division of labour or specialisation of functions, and, in the majority of cases, no machinery or power. Work is heavy; craftsmanship fastidious; methods patient, laborious and slow; discipline slack or absent. Relations are human, not mechanical. There is much physical exertion, and little nervous strain. The product is often of singular simplicity and beauty. There is a curious contrast between the slovenliness of Chinese workmanship on western patterns—windows that will not open and doors that will not shut—and the admirable fitness and precision of the wares which it makes by methods native to its genius to meet the needs of common life. It is as though, when he abandoned tradition, the craftsman lost all standards, and when he followed it, were infallible.

An illustration of the characteristics of this type of organisation is given by the handicraft industries of Peiping, described in the valuable books of Mr. Gamble and Mr. Burgess.[2] The thirty-four gilds of that city included, in 1920, some 107,000 members, consisting of masters, journeymen and apprentices, out of a total population of something over 800,000. The membership of the twenty-five among them for which

---

[1] J. B. Tayler, *The Hopei Pottery Industry and the Problem of Modernisation*, and D. K. Lieu, *China's Industries and Finance*.

[2] S. B. Gamble and J. S. Burgess, *Peking: A Social Survey* (1921), Chap. VIII and (for statistics) Appx. VI, p. 430; Burgess, *The Guilds of Peking* (1928).

complete figures are available was just over 90,000, of whom
about 10,000, or 11·4 per cent, were masters, 58,000, or 64 per
cent, journeymen, and 22,000, or 24·6 per cent, apprentices.
The number of journeymen and apprentices per master
ranged from 0·9 in the case of the shoe-makers, and 1·8 in
that of the jade-makers, to 73·5 among the carpet-makers,
and 106·6 among the silk-dyers. But the undertakings were
usually small, and sometimes minute: in ten out of these
twenty-five crafts the number of journeymen and apprentices
per master was less than ten, and in only five over twenty.
Equally significant was the general reliance on apprentice
labour: in eighteen out of the twenty-five trades there were less
than four journeymen to one apprentice, and in eleven less than
three, while, as already stated, apprentices formed almost a
quarter of the total membership. The limitation of apprentices,
which plays so large a part in the gild and early trade union
history of Europe, has not apparently been among the rules
generally enforced by the gilds of China.

Apart from provincial associations called by the same name,
and formed of members belonging to one province to protect
their interests when domiciled in another, the gilds of China
have hitherto consisted partly of traders, partly of craftsmen,
and most commonly, perhaps, of both.[1] In practice, as is
natural when the producer of wares is also their salesman, the
two types are often indistinguishable. Their number in China
as a whole is uncertain, but must run into several thousand.
In Canton alone there are stated to be upwards of a hundred,
covering every occupation from tailoring and shoe-making to
pig-killing, pawnbroking and coffin-making; controlling prices,
wages and hours; arbitrating between members and customers; and, in case of necessity, bringing pressure to bear on
officials and public authorities.

[1] For Chinese gilds see Gamble and Burgess, *op. cit.*, and Burgess, *op. cit.*; *China,
A Commercial and Industrial Handbook* (Washington, 1926), pp. 370–376; K. A. Witt-
fogel, *Wirtschaft und Gesellschaft Chinas* (Leipzig, 1931), pp. 573 *et seq.*; H. D. Fong,
Chinese Gilds Old and New, in the *Chinese Students' Monthly*, April, 1928; and for
earlier information, H. B. Morse, *The Gilds of China*, 1909; F. W. Williams, *Chinese
and Mediaeval Gilds*, in the *Yale Review*, November, 1892; and *China Imperial
Customs: Decennial Reports*, 1892–1901.

In their traditionalist technique, their multitude of little employers, and their strict corporate organisation, with its patron saints and festivals, and its combination of economic, social and religious functions, the handicrafts of China have naturally reminded observers of mediaeval misteries and fraternities. The resemblance is genuine; but the difference, perhaps, is not less significant. If the gilds by which Chinese crafts were till recently governed recall those of the West in their protective devices, their hatred of competition, and an exclusiveness so jealous that, in some cases, only the relatives of masters could be apprenticed to the trade, they are contrasted with them by their detachment from the larger political interests of the community surrounding them. They protected their members against individual exactions and personal tyranny; but, while powerful to resist the abuses of authority, they were impotent to remove the causes which produced them. The process by which, in parts of Europe, the gild evolved from a humble association of craftsmen into an organ impinging on governments, and, at times, controlling them, is a chapter that is missing from the history of China.

No Etienne Boileau has compiled a *Livre des Mestiers* of Chinese trades. The number and organisation of these handicraft industries is a matter for speculation. Twenty years hence, if not sooner, it will be too late to explore them; for, important as they still are in most parts of the country, it is clear that, year by year, their hold is weakening. The force which is undermining them is less the direct competition of factory production than the encroachment of a type of organisation which has always existed, but which attains new dimensions as commerce expands and markets widen. Its characteristic is that the craftsman, while continuing to produce by the traditional processes in a workshop or in his home, ceases to deal directly with the market, and is employed on commission by a merchant capitalist. Described by different names by different authorities, it may be regarded either as the last phase in the evolution of the small master, or as a stage of capitalism preceding that of factory industry.

One form which this arrangement assumes has long been widely diffused in rural districts. It is the cottage industry which was characteristic of the textile trades in all European countries before the Industrial Revolution, and is found in some of them to-day. Cotton-weaving, hosiery-knitting, the spinning of yarn for carpets, the preparation of silk for factories, the working of bamboo, embroidery, paper-making from straw, hair-net making, incense and fire-cracker making, the manufacture of umbrellas, shoes and straw hats, often as by-employments to agriculture, occupy a large number of persons of both sexes, working sometimes at home, sometimes in small workshops, to the order of merchants.

It is naturally in localities where density of population or a large export trade creates a mass demand that this type of organisation expands most easily, and it is rapidly ousting the independent master in the larger towns. An example of it, as it exists in the second industrial city of China, is supplied by the admirable studies of the industries of Tientsin produced by the Nankai University Committee on Social and Economic Research. Of the 303 carpet-making firms, with 11,568 workers, in that city, some manufacture on their own account; some work for a wholesale house, which pays them per square foot of carpet produced; others pass, according to the state of trade, from one category to the other. In the manufacture of hosiery, where materials, and sometimes machines, are purchased by the small master, or advanced to them by the merchant, and in the rayon and cotton weaving industries, similar methods obtain. The undertakings vary in size from a handful employing 100 workers, or more, to the great majority, which employ less than 30, and whose investment of capital is of the minutest.[1] The tools used, apart from the knitting machines, often acquired on credit, are hand-looms of a primitive character. The workshop is often little more than a barn or shed, in which meals are taken in the intervals of work, and which serves as a

[1] H. D. Fong, *The Tientsin Carpet Industry* (1929); *Rayon and Cotton Weaving in Tientsin* (1930); *Hosiery Knitting in Tientsin* (1930). All published by the Nankai University Committee on Social and Economic Research, Tientsin.

[Continued on page 118

dormitory to the workers at night. The nucleus of the business
is the labour of the family, supplemented, when the demand
increases, by unpaid apprentices or hired wage-earners,[1] who

Continuation of Note]

Number of Workers per Establishment	Number of Establishments		Capital per Establishment (in Mexican Dollars)	Number of Establishments	
(i) *Carpet Making*	Number	Per Cent		Number	Per Cent
1 to 10	56	18·5	1 to 100	77	26·3
11 to 20	96	31·7	101 to 200	73	24·9
21 to 30	46	15·2	201 to 300	43	14·7
31 to 40	24	7·9	301 to 400	19	6·5
41 to 50	26	8·6	401 to 500	39	13·3
51 to 100	33	10·8	501 to 1,000	19	6·5
Above 100	22	7·3	Above 1,000	23	7·8
Total	303	100·0	Total ..	293	100·0
(ii) *Rayon and Cotton Weaving*					
1 to 10	82	25·1	1 to 100	24	7·5
11 to 20	109	33·4	101 to 200	31	9·6
21 to 30	53	16·2	201 to 300	30	9·3
31 to 40	44	13·5	301 to 400	11	3·4
41 to 50	17	5·2	401 to 500	65	20·2
51 to 100	15	4·5	501 to 1,000	57	17·7
Above 100	7	2·1	Above 1,000	104	32·3
Total	327	100·0	Total ..	322	100·0
(iii) *Hosiery Knitting*					
1 to 10	96	64·4	1 to 100	22	14·6
11 to 20	39	26·2	101 to 200	21	14·1
21 to 30	9	6·1	201 to 300	21	14·0
31 to 40	2	1·3	301 to 400	6	4·0
41 to 50	1	0·7	401 to 500	33	22·0
Above 50	2	1·3	501 to 1,000	20	13·3
			Above 1,000	27	18·0
Total	149	100·0	Total ..	150	100·0

[1] See H. D. Fong, *Hosiery Knitting in Tientsin*, p. 63, where the figures for the
three trades are grouped as follows:

Trade	Apprentices		Journeymen		Total
	Number	Per Cent	Number	Per Cent	
Carpet Making ..	3,262	28	8,306	72	11,568
Rayon and Cotton Weaving	5,117	65	2,756	35	7,873
Hosiery Knitting ..	1,159	72	451	28	1,610
Total	9,538	45	11,513	55	21,051

for the time become part of it. Nor are such conditions peculiar to Tientsin or to the industries mentioned. The wanderer in a Chinese city or village can hardly escape from the clack of the looms, and can watch through doors opening on the street small groups of workers weaving cotton, making carpets or winding silk.

The personnel of these small industries is large compared with that employed in factories, but it is small in comparison with the total population engaged in urban industry. Machinery being scanty, human energy is exploited in its place. In China, as in Europe to the end of the eighteenth century, work is done by man-power which in industrialised countries is performed by steam or electricity. The first sensation of a visitor to a Chinese city is one of suffocation beneath a torrent of human beings, straining at manual labour or clamouring to be given it.

Statistics are unobtainable. Belonging to no definite class, this great army of labourers has never been classified. They are the "others" or "unknown," who account for anything from 5 to 20 per cent of such local occupational censuses as have been taken. Such evidence as is available shows that the number of workers required to produce a given output is, judged by western standards, almost fantastically high; in mining, for example, it has been estimated that, owing to the absence of machinery, the native mines, while employing over 60 per cent of the workers in the industry, produce only 30 to 40 per cent of the coal raised,[1] and that the output per worker is barely a fifth of that of miners in Great Britain, who are working deeper seams, with a longer journey to the coal face, and a larger proportion of oncost workers. The same is true of quarrying, digging clay, salt-making, building and works of construction, navvying and road repairing, the raising and lowering of water for irrigating the fields, which is done by treadles worked by human feet or by hand, and, indeed, of almost all kinds

[1] Torgasheff, *Mining Labour in China* (*Chinese Economic Journal*, Vol. VI, No. 4); H. F. Bain, *Ores and Industry in the Far East*, p. 185; L. K. Tao and S. H. Lin, *Industry and Labour in China* (Bureau of Social Research, Peiping).

of heavy work. Capital is dear, and labour, being cheap, is employed instead of it. As a consequence, the proportion of unskilled workers, whose sole qualification is muscular strength, to the total industrial population is, to western eyes, abnormally large. There can be few countries which squander admirable human resources with the same prodigality.

A trite, but instructive, example is that of transport. Except in a small area in the east, the railway mileage is negligible. The use of motor transport is in its infancy—the total number of motor vehicles in operation in 1929 was stated to be less than 30,000, of which one-third were to be found in the Foreign Concessions at Shanghai.[1] Horses, in many parts of the country, are hardly employed; nor are the roads of a kind to permit regular traffic by cart. Hence, while the cost of transport is so crushing as to cripple both agriculture and manufacturing industry, human labour continues to be employed to carry it on, because, in the conditions of to-day, there is nothing which is cheaper. In addition to some 153,000 railway and 27,000 postal workers, there are dock labourers, labourers carrying wares by pole, labourers loaded with wares on their shoulders, an unnumbered army of wheelbarrow men, muleteers, and, for the transport of persons, rickshaw pullers, estimated to amount in seven cities alone to over 130,000,[2] not to mention sedan-chair carriers. The statement that 20 per cent of the population of China is engaged in transport is, no doubt, an exaggeration; but it is not wholly unplausible. It is possible to spend a morning in the principal streets of a city with a population of over a quarter of a million persons, and to see one motor-lorry filled with soldiers, two carts drawn by ponies too small for them, and an almost unbroken procession of human beings moving bales and packing cases from one end of it to the other.

This army of unskilled urban workers is swollen by immi-

[1] *Motor Highways in China*, by A. Viola Smith (U.S. Department of Commerce, Washington, 1929).
[2] *Chinese Economic Journal*, Vol. VII, No. 7, July, 1930 (*Rickshaws in China*, by Fang Fu-an).

grants from rural districts. Migration is partly seasonal: Shanghai, for example, is said to receive several thousand agricultural workers each winter, of whom some remain, but the majority leave on the return of spring. It is partly the result of exceptional misfortune—famine, civil war and banditry; in conditions such as those of the last ten years, the victims of these evils crowd into towns and squat on a vacant plot within the vast area included in the walls of most Chinese cities. When work is a speculation, there can be no sharp division between the workers and the workless. For large numbers of the worst situated among them, half-employment is the rule, so that employed and unemployed melt into each other. The more fortunate secure a succession of jobs with fair regularity while they continue to be in the prime of their strength, but they break down young. The less fortunate, the weak and the elderly, eke out a living by an occasional stroke of luck, and are preserved from starvation by the family communism which gives the individual a recognised claim on the resources of the group. Little, however, can be said as to this floating population of casual workers, for little is known about it. The problem of factory labour in China is grave, but at present it is small compared with that of the coolie. It is surprising that, when so much attention is rightly concentrated on the first, so little that is of value should have been written on the second.

(ii)

THE GROWTH OF CAPITALIST INDUSTRY

The industrial system characteristic of China is that which predominated in most regions of the West till the nineteenth century. In parts of the country this traditional order no longer stands alone. For more than a generation a new type of economic technique and industrial structure has been developing on the fringe of a society based on handicraft methods and small productive units.

The significance of this movement is easily exaggerated and easily underestimated. The part played in China by machinery, power, the mass organisation of production, and the financial mechanism which these phenomena imply, has greatly increased in the last quarter of a century; but, compared with its importance in Europe and America, it is still inconsiderable. The materials for a detailed account of the progress of industrialisation are scanty and unreliable. In Table I in the Appendix an attempt is made to indicate the state of its development at different dates between 1896 and 1930.

Apart from the State arsenals, the great industry hardly existed in China before 1890.[1] The first cotton mills were established in that year. A short railway line, which was almost immediately destroyed, had been opened in 1876, and a second was built between 1880 and 1894; but railway construction on a substantial scale did not begin till after the Sino-Japanese War. The Treaty of Shimonoseiki, which permitted foreigners to establish industrial plants in treaty ports, gave a new impetus to the development of manufacturing industry. Even in 1910, however, there were, as far as is known, only 4,500 miles of railway, 26 cotton mills, and 31 modern flour mills, in the whole country. The war of 1914–1918, by cutting off foreign supplies, and giving Chinese producers a monopoly of the home market, opened a new era. The result was a rapid expansion of industry in China; and, though hampered by civil disorder, forced loans and high taxation, and currency difficulties, growth continued between 1918 and 1930. If the figures given in Table I of the Appendix are approximately correct, the output of coal in 1929 was 79 per cent above that of 1913; the railway mileage was about 76 per cent higher; and

---

[1] There were, however, certain earlier developments. The first steamship was built by a Chinese company in 1862. The China Merchants' Steam Navigation Company was organised in 1872. The first rice-cleaning mill was established in Shanghai in 1863, the first silk filature in 1873, the first modern coal mine in 1878, and the first iron and steel works in 1890. For these, and other particulars, I am indebted to the excellent study by Professor H. D. Fong, *China's Industrialisation, a Statistical Survey* (Shanghai, 1931).

motor-roads, which hardly existed before 1920, had been considerably extended. The development of machine production is
shown by the increase in the imports of machinery and raw cotton, and in the number of cotton mills and factories. The rapid
growth in the number of modern banks is equally significant.[1]

As in the case of most countries in the first phase of the
Industrial Revolution, it is the manufacturing, not the extractive industries, which have expanded most rapidly. Judged by
western standards, the mining and metallurgical industries of
China are not at present considerable. Her output of coal was
in 1928 about one-tenth of that of Great Britain; and, apart
from two concerns, which between them accounted for over
one-third of it, the majority of undertakings were small, only
41 producing over 5,000 tons a year, and only 17 over 100,000
tons. Her iron and steel industries are even less developed. The
production of iron ore in 1928 was 2,003,800 tons, of which
73 per cent came from eight modern mines, the largest with
an output of 540,000 tons. She has nine modern iron-works,
with an annual capacity of approximately 967,400 tons of
pig-iron and 110,000 tons of steel; but the industry has suffered
severely from economic depression and civil disorder, and in
1928, the last year for which figures are available, only four
were working. A point of capital importance, both for the
economic and the political future of China, is the fact that,
backward as her heavy industries are, they are largely outside
Chinese control. Foreign interests fastened on her mineral
resources, before she realised their importance or was prepared to develop them by modern methods. The result is
that some 56 per cent of her coal output is raised by foreign
undertakings, that approximately 82 per cent of her small
iron deposits are the property of Japanese concerns, and that
a large proportion of her output of ore is exported to
Japan. In a reasonable world such conditions might not
matter; with the world as it is they matter very much. It

---

[1] Figures later than 1925 appear not to be available. In that year there were
(in addition to 43 foreign and 20 Sino-foreign banks) 141 Chinese banks, of which
93 had been established in or after 1919 (see Fong, *op. cit.*, pp. 28–29).

is as though the South Wales coal-field and the Yorkshire steel industry had passed in the nineteenth century into alien ownership.[1]

Manufactures, in particular the textile industries, are the field in which modernisation has proceeded furthest, though the movement, even here, is still in its infancy. Figures purporting to show the number of factories, capital invested, workers employed, and value of product turned out, in certain cities and provinces, were published by the Ministry of Industries at the end of 1930.[2] Provinces disturbed by war, or those in which communications are so bad as to prevent information being obtained, were not included in them. The regions represented were those of the Eastern Coast, the Lower Yangtze valley and Manchuria. Though they relate only to twenty-nine cities and are not exhaustive even for them, they give some idea of the scale and distribution of factory industry in the majority of the most economically advanced parts of China,[3] and are accordingly summarised in Tables II to V in the Appendix.

It will be seen from these Tables, both that, in the areas represented, the number of factories officially known to exist grew just under three times between 1920 and 1930, and that, even when allowance is made for the very elastic

---

[1] For figures of output and undertakings, see Fong, *op. cit.*, pp. 14–16, and for concerns in foreign ownership, L. K. Tao and S. H. Lin, *op. cit.* pp. 11–14, The latter gives the following figures of coal production by different classes of mines :

	1928 Production (Thousand Tons)	Per Cent
Modern mines operated with foreign capital ..	14,117	56·3
Modern mines operated with Chinese capital ..	3,169	12·6
Chinese mines operated by primitive methods..	7,805	31·1
Total	25,091	100·0

[2] *General Statistics of Factories in China*, 1930.
[3] For a criticism of the figures, see Fong, *op. cit.*, p. 17. While some of the provinces not represented have few, if any, industrial undertakings of a modern type, others have a considerable number. The most noticeable omission from the return is Tientsin.

definition of the word "factory"[1] given in the Report, it is still

[1] The word "factory" is a source of endless confusion to the student of Chinese industrial conditions, owing to the different senses in which it is used. In the figures issued by the Department of Agriculture and Commerce, 1912–20, a factory was defined as a manufacturing establishment with seven or more persons, with the result that numerous small workshops were returned as factories. The Factory Law promulgated on December 30, 1929 (see below, pp. 154–156), stated that it was to apply to "all factories, driven by steam, gas, electricity or water power, regularly employing workers 30 or more in number." In the report of 1930, the figures relate to establishments employing 30 or more workers, but no reference is made to power. In practice the word "factory" is applied to establishments which would not be described as factories in Europe or America. See *The Chinese Economic Bulletin*, January 5, 1929, for a list of 349 factories in Chekiang in 1928, as follows:

Establishments		Total Number of Workers	Average Number per Factory
3 Cotton yarn factories	.. ..	3,930	1,310
76 Silk filatures		15,998	205
37 Cotton cloth factories		4,129	111
39 Hosiery factories		1,505	38
7 Mat factories ..	.. ..	467	67
15 Iron works		504	33
17 Paper factories		826	46
15 Soap and candle factories ..	..	171	11
8 Tanneries		41	5
16 Rice-husking factories ..	..	128	8
76 Electric houses		466	6
8 Canneries		218	27
4 Match factories		2,935	733
28 Other factories		623	22

In Shanghai, according to the Social Affairs Bureau, 1,071 out of 1,498 factories, or 71 per cent, had in 1928 less than 90 workers, and 312, or 20 per cent, less than 30 workers. The industries in which more than 90 workers were employed per factory were the following:

Establishments		Total Number of Workers	Average Number per Factory
55 Cotton-spinning factories	.. ..	94,342	1,715
90 Silk-reeling factories ..	.. ..	52,463	583
7 Match factories ..	.. ..	2,737	391
3 Clothing factories ..	.. ..	1,050	350
1 Egg-preserving factory ..	..	287	287
8 Water and electricity works ..	..	1,781	223
13 Paper factories ..	.. ..	2,193	169
12 Flour mills	.. ..	1,871	156
5 Cotton-ginning factories	.. ..	739	142
69 Cigarette factories ..	..	9,478	137
46 Silk-weaving factories	..	6,262	136
12 Oil-pressing mills ..	.. ..	1,501	125
7 Wool-weaving factories	.. ..	828	118
99 Cotton-weaving factories	.. ..	9,327	94

See, on the whole subject, H. D. Fong, *op. cit.*, from whom the above figures are taken.

surprisingly small. It is difficult to believe that, in the towns concerned, the number of undertakings with 30 workers or more is only 1,975, and the number in China as a whole must obviously be larger. Since, however, these towns include the majority of the most important industrial centres, with the exception of Tientsin, it is possibly not very much larger; and, even if it were multiplied by three, the factories in China would still be noticeably few. It is impossible to state the number of workers engaged in factory industry. The official figures of those employed in 29 towns is 1,204,318.[1] Other estimates put them, in China as a whole, at 1,400,000 to 1,500,000; no one appears to have estimated them at above 2,500,000.[2] Accuracy is impossible, but it is clear that, apart from a few exceptional cities, they form a small minority of the total industrial population.

The establishments represented in the official figures include great undertakings, such as cotton mills, with 2,000 or more employees, and tiny concerns. Small as is the number of those classed as factories, large-scale production, as the words are understood in most western countries, is far rarer. The principal industries in which it exists are coal, iron and steel, cotton and silk, flour-milling, oil-milling, match-making, soap-making, and electric light and power. Though, of course, isolated businesses in other industries have introduced modern methods, the undertakings which may be described as thoroughly modernised in technique and organisation probably are not more, in the aggregate, than 2,500 to 3,000. Whatever view may be taken of the future, it will probably be agreed that the Industrial Revolution in China, if half a dozen cities be omitted, has at present hardly more than begun. In cotton-spinning—the industry which has passed most completely into the factory—her 127 mills are fewer in number, though, of

---

[1] See below pp. 198, 200.

[2] Nishikawa, *Labour Conditions in Central China*, estimates them at 1,400,000. *China, A Commercial and Industrial Handbook* (U.S. Department of Commerce, 1926, p. 268), gives 1,500,000; *The Chinese Labour Year Book*, 1928, p. 15, gives 1,460,000. See also C. F. Ma, *Notes on China's Labour Population* (*Chinese Economic Journal*, Vol. VII, No. 5, November, 1930), and Tao and Lin, *op. cit.*

course, far more efficient, than those which existed in England in 1795. Her output of coal is about equal to that produced by the latter country in 1820. Her consumption of iron per head of the population is probably about one-thirtieth of that of the world. Compared with the consumption of industrial Europe, and still more of the United States, it is almost negligible.

What is not less significant is the degree to which modern industry is confined to certain limited areas. Industrial China may be divided into three main regions—the ports, the hinterland served by railways and rivers, and the interior. In the first, industrial capitalism, historically a foreign importation, is of great, and, sometimes, of preponderant, importance; in the second, it is growing, but is still in its infancy; in the third, which is much the largest, though its impact from a distance is increasingly felt, it hardly exists as a localised force, with roots in the soil and a life of its own. The six provinces of Kiangsu, Liaoning, Hopei, Kwangtung, Shantung and Hupeh contain some 10 per cent of the area of China, and, perhaps, about 36 per cent of her total population. But they account for 92 per cent of her foreign trade, 53 per cent of her railways, 42 per cent of her motor roads, 64 per cent of her coal and iron-ore output, 93 per cent of the cotton yarn spun, 92 per cent of the silk reeled, 86 per cent of the oil pressed, and 87 per cent of the electric-power capacity. Of the 1,302 factories in the return quoted above, which came into existence in the decade 1920–30, 827, or two-thirds, were established in four cities—645 in Shanghai, 110 in Wusih, 38 in Hankow, and 34 in Dairen— and one-third were established in the rest of China. No less then 42 per cent of the 1,975 factories reported in 1930 were in Shanghai, while, of the 810 companies registered in the years 1928–29, 383, or 47 per cent, had their seat in that city, and another 101, or 12 per cent, in the province of Kiangsu in which it is situated.[1] The wider geographical diffusion of industrial enterprises in 1930, as compared with the situation obtaining in 1920, and still more in 1911, is a healthy symptom. It is evident, however, that they still tend to be concen-

[1] M. T. Z. Tyau, *Two Years of Nationalist China*, pp. 198–200.

trated in areas the conditions of which differ somewhat sharply
from those obtaining in the rest of the country.

Economic development does not lend itself to portrayal in
snap-shots. It is evident that an industrial civilisation of the
western type is in its infancy in China, and that conventional
pictures of a country in rapid process of modernisation are
absurdly overdrawn. But, granted that fact, her present
economic position is open, nevertheless, to more than one
interpretation. If the progress of modern industry is to be
measured by the general use of machinery and power, then
there is no country, except England, in which it is more than
a century old, and in most it is far younger. Once the ice is
broken, the current is apt to run, given the necessary conditions, with surprising rapidity. Germany was by 1900 one of
the greatest of industrial nations, the creator of two fundamental industries, and the leader in more; but her rise to that
position had taken place within less than a single lifetime. In
Prussia, for which alone adequate figures exist, 72 per cent of
the population was in 1850 rural, the output of coal less than
5,000,000 tons, the engines used for industrial purposes fewer
than 2,000, and the locomotives than 500, while, in her dependence on imports for most of her manufactured goods, she
bore some resemblance to China to-day. Japan modernised
her industrial system, on certain of its most important sides, in
less than a generation. From an overwhelmingly agricultural
country she had become by 1925 one in which 55 per cent of
the population lived in towns of more than 5,000.

In China herself, the great industry has struggled onto its
feet amid overwhelming difficulties. The effects of war, defective communications, scarcity of capital, political insecurity
and heavy taxation, which retarded economic development on
the continent of Europe during the first half of last century,
have in China paralysed it. They have been aggravated by
almost continuous internal disorder, the absence of any
government whose writ ran without question throughout the

country as a whole, the poverty of the agricultural population, a social environment set in the mould of the past and intractable to change, currency and exchange difficulties, the control by foreign interests of key positions in finance, transport and commerce, and the fact that China's limited mineral resources are to a considerable extent exploited by foreign firms, which ship part of the product abroad to become the basis of manufacturing industries in countries other than China. A native capitalism is in process of development, which may or may not be an improvement on the imported article. It is still the case, however, that over one-quarter of China's railway mileage, over three-quarters of her iron ore, mines producing more than half her output of coal, more than half the capital invested in cotton mills, and a smaller but not negligible proportion of that invested in oil mills, flour mills, tobacco factories, motor factories and banks is in the hands of foreigners. Dr. Sun Yat-sen's description of China as a colony is, from an economic point of view, not inappropriate.[1]

What is surprising in such circumstances, it may reasonably be argued, is not that the modernisation of industry has taken place gradually, and in isolated areas, but that it has taken place at all. The point of importance is not the situation which exists in China in 1931, but the direction in which her economic life is likely to move in the next half-century. Is it probable that an industrial system based on power and machinery will develop in China, not merely as an exotic flourishing in a few exceptional regions, but as a mature and spontaneous growth which is widely diffused? If such a development takes place, what advantages may it be expected to offer, and what problems will it produce? Is it possible to accelerate, direct or control it in the general interest of the nation as a whole?

The foundations of modern industry are both material and psychological. It depends partly on the command of the neces-

[1] *San Min Chu I*, trans. by Frank W. Price, 1931. For coal and iron, see above, pp. 123–124; railways, J. E. Baker, *Explaining China*, p. 217; cotton mills, L. K. Tao and S. H. Lin, *op. cit.*, pp. 16–17; oil mills, flour mills, tobacco and match factories, *The Manchuria Year Book* (Tokyo, 1931), pp. 117–131; banks, Fong, *op. cit.*, pp. 28–29.

sary natural resources, partly on scientific knowledge, partly
on the existence of habits and institutions which enable the
knowledge to be applied and the resources to be exploited.
Science, and the technology based upon science, are now an
international possession, accessible to all. On the legal and
political conditions of economic progress it is needless to
dwell. What makes modern industry is ultimately not the
machine, but the brains which use it, and the institutional
framework which enables it to be used. It is a social product,
which owes as much to the jurist as to the inventor. To regard
it as an ingenious contrivance, like a mechanical toy, or the
gilded clocks in the museum at Peiping made by London
jewellers for the amusement of Chinese emperors, which a
country can import to suit its fancy, irrespective of the character of the environment in which the new technique is to
function, is naïve to the point of absurdity. It is like supposing
that, in order to acclimatise Chinese script in the West, it
would be sufficient to introduce Chinese brushes and ink. But
institutions are plastic and habits change; both have altered
profoundly in China in the course of a generation. A nation
which wills the end is not likely, as far as this aspect of the
problem is concerned, to be embarrassed indefinitely through
lack of means. If China desires to modernise her industry, it is
improbable that she will continue for long to be baulked
merely by the existence of psychological obstacles.

Does she genuinely desire it? Or is her real aim a more
subtle one—to use western technique as an instrument, while
resisting domination by the mentality behind it? Only a
Chinese can say, and, perhaps, not even he. No task is more
difficult than to strike a just balance between the forces making
for change, forces active and vocal, and the vast reserves of
sagacious experience to which change must be accommodated.
As one reads official programmes, and listens to rhapsodies on
the magic of modern industry, one could fancy oneself back
in the England of 1850 or the America of 1920. It is possible
that there is a section of Chinese opinion, incredible though
it seems, whose enthusiasm for Mr. Ford is as innocent of

reservations as its utterances would suggest. It is possible, but not probable. In a people so mature and wary as the Chinese there are depths not easily sounded; its mind is disclosed less in its words than in its life. China is not a primitive society to be swept off her feet by the glitter and swirl of alluring novelties. Her culture is autonomous, her conception of the life proper to civilized man exacting, and her own. She has a profound sense of her own identity, an instinctive awareness of the new elements which she can absorb without ceasing to be herself, which makes abrupt changes of direction and irrevocable commitments repugnant to her genius.

Chinese who applaud the triumphs of the machine rarely mean what the West means when it uses the same phrases. The latter hails it as a master, the former accept it as a servant. When they reflect on the weakness of their own country in the face of foreign Powers, they feel like a giant outwitted by a dwarf. They admire the devices which give success to the barbarian, as a European may admire the skill of a native tracker who follows game through the bush, or kindles a camp fire by rubbing sticks. To neutralise his capacity for mischief, so prodigious and incalculable, and gain what good he has to offer, they must master his tricks. But tricks, after all, are but tricks; means are means, and nothing more. Apart from a handful of ex-students educated in America, most Chinese would as little dream of succumbing to the philosophy of the West, and endorsing its ends, as the European of exchanging his life for that of the bushman.

Their reactions to industrialism are, consequently, not simple and decided, but complex and hesitating. They would take the thing, for it is useful, but they would take it on their own terms; wise men, who know good and evil, do not surrender their souls. It is a question, in short, not of acceptance or imitation, but of adaptation and adjustment. Adjustment demands time, and one reason for the slow advance of economic change in China, compared with its swift progress in Japan, is psychological. It is that an interval is required in which the alien elements can be digested and assimilated. In the process of assimilation those elements themselves undergo a subtle sublimation. Fused with their Chinese environment, they change their chemistry; they take up new properties, which blend with and transform them. Whether, thus qualified and subdued, capitalist industry will retain the economic qualities which constitute its attraction, only time can show; but one prophecy may be hazarded. It is that, like all other movements which have been imported from abroad and acclimatised in China, it will be propagated in a Chinese version or not at all.

The question of natural resources is on a different plane. The most important of them are coal, iron, oil and water-power. As far as the first three are concerned, the tendency of recent work has been to reduce the estimates formerly advanced of China's mineral endowments. According to the figures of Dr. Wong,[1] the director of the Geological Survey, her known coal resources are 23,435,000,000 tons in seams of not less than one metre in thickness at a depth not exceeding 100 metres, with, possibly, an additional 17,000,000,000 to 27,000,000,000 tons in thinner seams and at a greater depth. If these figures are correct, China's known coal resources are slightly less than twice those of France, and about equal to those of Czecho-Slovakia; while, if the reserves which may exist, but are not yet in sight, are included, the total is approximately the same as the known resources of Great Britain. Much of the coal, it must be remembered, is inconveniently situated, and only part of it is fit for coking; the only fields likely to supply coal suitable for metallurgical purposes are stated to be those of Hopei, Fengtien and Shansi in the north, and Kwangsi in the south. China's supplies of iron are much more scanty: according to the estimate of the Chinese Geological Survey,[2] her deposits amount to 979,000,000 tons, or, possibly, something over 2 tons per head of population, compared with 37·9 tons in the United States. So far as is known, she has no important oil resources. The possibilities of hydro-electric energy have still to be fully explored. It seems possible that water-power might be used on a considerable

[1] Quoted Bain, *Ores and Industry in the Far East.*   [2] *Ibid.*

scale in parts of the south. While the materials for any decided judgment do not yet exist, scientists seem at present to speak with greater hesitation than politicians of the part which it is likely to play in the future economic development of the country.

If the annual output of coal in China were increased five-fold, her resources, actual and potential, would last for something over 400 years, though with steeply rising costs before the end of the period. As far as the visible future is concerned, the limiting factor is not coal, but iron. At the rate of consumption prevailing in the United States, China's reserves of ore, it has been remarked, would be exhausted in a few years. This disability is serious, but its consequences are less crushing, it might plausibly be urged, than such a statement at first suggests. For one thing, any considerable increase in consumption must necessarily be gradual, and can proceed some way before stringency is felt. For another, the United States, with its vast mineral resources, employs iron and steel for a multitude of purposes for which countries less rich in them employ other materials. Prosperity does not depend on using iron and steel with the utmost possible profusion, but on using them for those objects for which they are necessary, and, in the case of a nation whose supplies are small, on being careful to use them for nothing else. In the third place, since over three-quarters of the iron ore raised in China is produced by firms under foreign control, it is economically possible for her, given the necessary political arrangements, to increase her own consumption, without thereby accelerating the depletion of her reserves. In the fourth place, the possibility of supplementing domestic supplies by foreign imports, if improbable in any near future, is not out of the question. It is known that considerable reserves of iron ore exist in the Philippines. Since China has the greatest coal resources of the East, it is conceivable that the former may in time be brought to the latter.

Some weight, no doubt, must be given to such considerations. The fact remains, however, that the growth of an iron and steel industry of considerable dimensions is hardly possible in China. She may create one on a scale sufficient to meet her most urgent needs, but natural limitations will prevent it from becoming of more than local importance. If that view is correct, the conclusion to be drawn from it is not that, when other pre-requisites exist—which at present they do not—China cannot develop large-scale manufactures with a modern technique, but merely that the field in which the greatest developments are to be expected is not that of the heavy industry. She requires the products of the latter for certain indispensable purposes; but, in view of her deficiency of iron ore, she will be prudent to reserve them for those purposes alone.

Apart from iron and steel, the possibilities open to her remain substantial. In discussions by Chinese economists of the economic future of their country, the nation most commonly cited as an index, against which to measure her economic stature and its possible growth, appears to be the United States. Few comparisons could be less felicitous. In reality, if parallels are to be sought in other parts of the world, a less inapt analogy than that with America or Germany would be with France before 1914. In pre-war France, owing partly to the inadequacy of her mineral resources, the output of coal, in particular coking coal, and of iron and steel, was small compared with that both of those countries and of Great Britain. The industries in which she was pre-eminent, and which, in spite of the impressive expansion of her iron and steel production during the last decade, are still, perhaps, most characteristic of her genius, were those in which ingenuity, taste, dexterity, rather than the disciplined routine of mass production, were the conditions of success. More than any other country, she has known how to make the best both of the present and of the past, and has grafted the great industry on to her traditional social organisation, without as yet undermining the latter.

No analogy of the kind can, of course, be pressed far. The lines on which machine industry has so far proceeded in China suggest, however, that her future may lie in the development of manufactures based less on the domestic production of a large output of iron and steel than on cheap power, manual skill, and such imports of machinery as are needed to supply requirements that cannot be met at home. Provided that she can export sufficient to purchase the latter in the quantity needed, an expansion of secondary, rather than of primary, industries is neither, on a long view, impracticable, nor a ground for regret.

The disease of young China is its fever for imitation, and in programmes of industrial reconstruction it rages unchecked. Designed for America, for Europe, for the moon, for anywhere except the unhappy country on whose attention they are pressed, they rehearse impossibilities with dreadful monotony, as though mere persistence in repetition could convert fancies into facts. The course of wisdom in economic affairs is precisely the opposite. It is to "lead from strength." An intelligent nation need not copy slavishly the methods of other countries. It will discover in what its own peculiar advantages consist, and, instead of merely reproducing what is already done effectively elsewhere, will concentrate its efforts on doing what elsewhere is not done so well, or not done at all. China, it may be suggested, will make a profound mistake if she is so much impressed by the industrial achievements of America and Europe as merely to ape them, instead of striking out her own line for herself. She must start from the foundations of economic enterprise which already exist, expand those industries which, because she is best suited for them, offer the best conditions, and develop the assets which she already possesses.

Nor are such assets difficult to discover. China possesses a laborious and intelligent population, with unusual gifts for qualitative production; its most serious economic defect—a very grave one—is that, owing to its abundance, human labour is cheap, with the result that the introduction of machinery, which, had labour been dearer, would have taken place long ago, has been discouraged. She has valuable raw materials, which, owing to primitive methods of cultivation and preparation, are less valuable than they should be. Given the development of her coal industry, she may have cheap power. She already manufactures by modern methods a large output of goods which a generation ago were produced by hand, so that, as far as the immediate future is concerned, her problem is less to introduce new industries than to expand those of which the nucleus is already in existence. The character of her foreign trade, which—like that of most countries in the first phase of industrial development—is largely an exchange of raw materials and foodstuffs for manufactured imports, permits her, as her industry develops, to replace part of the latter by domestic products. She has a market at home which at present, owing to the absence of communications and to the low standard of life of the rural population, has a small effective demand, but which, given the improvement of transport and agriculture, is potentially large.

In such circumstances, if she cannot do a tithe—no country could—of what is proposed by enthusiastic politicians, she can, nevertheless, do much. It is difficult to believe that she cannot, for example, work up her raw silk and raw wool at home, instead of exporting them to be manufactured abroad; grow fruit and can it, instead of importing canned fruit from California; deal with her eggs in her own egg factories, instead of leaving the profits of exporting them to foreign concerns, and develop other industries based on agriculture; multiply her flour mills, oil mills and cement works; supply her own railway materials and electrical plant; carry further the substitution, which she has already begun, of Chinese cottons for piece-goods imported from Great Britain and Japan; and create the nucleus, at least, of a Chinese mercantile marine. Since she is never likely to be industrialised in the same sense as the United States, Germany or Great Britain, it is needless to inquire whether that type of civilisation possesses all the virtues with which Chinese politeness is accustomed to credit it. But it is paradoxical to suppose that, if she chooses to take the necessary steps—which at present she has not—she cannot greatly increase both her production of manufactures and the population employed in manufacturing industries.

The long view is one thing, the short another. Whether the space between them is to be measured by decades or by centuries, a stranger cannot say. The conditions of economic progress—peace; cheap and easy communications; a uniform and stable currency; the ruthless curtailment of military expenditure; the widest possible diffusion of education among all sections of the population; the formation of a body of competent technicians; reasonable sense and honesty in the management of affairs of state and of corporate undertakings; the improvement of agriculture and, thereby, of the home market; measures to prevent the exploitation of the cheap labour which is the curse of Chinese industry and a perpetual clog upon the improvement of its technique—such commonplaces are as familiar in China as in the West. The difference between them appears to be that, while parts of the latter are relapsing into poverty by destroying some of these prerequisites of prosperity, China remains in poverty through the slow growth of all of them.

An observer may suspect that the political and social impediments to her industrial development will not be permanent, but he has no means of gauging the rate of their disappearance. The measures most urgently needed are hardly open to dispute. The localisation of manufacturing industry in the China of to-day recalls that which existed in America a century and a half ago. It clings to the eastern coast, and rarely ventures into the precarious world that lies beyond the hinterland of the ports and rivers. A posture so unnatural cramps and distorts the economic and political growth of the country which suffers it. It is as though the blood which should circulate through the body were confined by a ligature within a single limb. Capital which should fertilise the resources of undeveloped areas is immobilised in a few great cities; the economic methods and social conditions of the thirteenth century continue unchanged within a few hours of the twentieth; as in the Europe of the Middle Ages, the town fears and despises the country, the country suspects and dislikes the town. The China of the interior and the China of the eastern fringe form, in fact, separate organisms, which, in economic organisation and intellectual habits, are still strangers to each other. The former is more remote from the latter, in all but geography, than is the latter from Europe.

The first remedy is simple. It is an immediate and continuous improvement of the means of communication. Transport, which is the condition of the progress of agriculture, is even more essential to the development of manufacturing industry. It is the readiest way—indeed, the only way—of breaking the vicious circle which binds economic stagnation to political disorder, and political disorder to economic stagnation. It is to the construction of railways, as finance makes it possible, and to the mobilisation of all available labour for the extension of roads, which, in a country congested with soldiers, is possible at once, that economic resources and constructive intelligence should first be devoted. Until an adequate system of transport exists, to talk of economic development is to play with words. Given such a system, disorder will be diminished. With the diminution of disorder, economic enterprise, instead of being tied to the coast, will spread into the interior, and, as it spreads, will create barriers against the return of disorder. The farmer will find new and more profitable markets within his reach. The growth of urban industry will increase the prosperity of agriculture. The increased prosperity of agriculture will in turn swell the effective demand for the products of industry.

The improvement of communications would naturally be accompanied by two other measures, one of which, indeed, is already being carried out. In the first place, in a country where manufacturing industries are struggling to their feet in the teeth of the competition of well-established rivals, a tariff on manufactured imports is a reasonable method of accelerating their development. China began her period of tariff autonomy on January 1, 1931. She marked the new era by imposing duties ranging from 5 per cent on ores and agricultural machinery up to 50 per cent on imports thought to compete seriously with domestic industries—$7\frac{1}{2}$ to 15 per cent on cotton yarn and piece-goods, 30 per cent on tea, 30 to 35 per cent on woollen goods and carpets, 40 per cent on matches, and 35 to 45 per cent on silk goods. Provided that the tariff is not indiscriminate but selective, that it chooses for protection those industries which can be expected, if sheltered, to develop, and that it is accompanied by steps to compel them, instead of dozing in agreeable torpor, to use the opportunity given them to put their house in order by overhauling their organisation and modernising their technique, it is likely to be worth its cost to the consumer.

The second requirement is at once more important and more difficult to satisfy. It is the adoption of some settled policy of industrial development, which rigorously excludes inessentials, aims at a small number of limited objectives, and is steadily carried out over a period of years. Programmes, like the majority of those hitherto advanced, which promise everything, necessarily effect nothing. They disperse interest and effort, instead of concentrating them; nor is it reasonable that, when capital is as scarce as it is in China to-day, it should be diverted into enterprises which, if laudable in themselves, are of secondary importance. What is needed now is not to add to the number of plans competing for attention, but to drop four-fifths of the proposals contained in those already put forward, and to make a serious attempt to secure that the remainder yield some practical result. It is, in short, what used to be called a Scheme of Priorities.

A scheme implies a competent authority to draft and carry it out. It is less than a year since such an authority was created. The National Economic Council, established in November, 1931, is the first step taken in China to bring reconstruction to earth. Its business will be to consider different proposals in relation to each other and to determine their relative importance, to draw up a plan of the work most urgently required, which can be set in hand during the next three years, to advise the Government, with due regard to the financial situation, as to the steps which can be taken to carry it out, and to arrange, when necessary, for the co-operation of foreign

experts. It will be required to decide, for example, on what
lines the urgent question of land reform is to be attacked and
in what areas it is to be first undertaken; what industries it is
most important to develop; on what lines Government assistance, if any, should be granted, and what form it should
assume; what steps shall be taken to cope with floods and
drought; in what directions and by what methods the transport system should be extended; how the organisation of the
national and provincial financial systems can be improved;
what measures can be adopted to spread more extensively
efficient systems of public health and education. Whether the
political situation of China will allow the Council to function
as intended, it is at present impossible to say. It is clear, however, that, even given favourable political conditions, it is
only through machinery of the kind that the planned economic
development, of which everyone talks, can be made a reality.

(iii)

PROBLEMS OF SOCIAL POLICY

The probable influence of the growth of manufacturing industry on the standard of general well-being is a different
question. It is needless to labour the truism that a mass attack
on nature, armed with weapons of precision, and carried out
by collective effort on a systematic plan, can win triumphs
unattainable by the skirmishes of individuals. If the "work
output" per head of population in China is estimated at less
than one-twentieth of that of the United States, the explanation is not that man toils harder in the latter than in the
former, but that machinery and power make his output
greater and his toil less hard.

Nothing is to be gained, however, by cherishing illusions,
and to invoke industrialisation as the magical formula which
will solve all problems is to court disappointment. The suggestion that it will result in an actual diminution of the rural

population, by causing a movement into manufactures of persons now employed in agriculture, is not likely to be realised. The first effect of the expansion of manufacturing industry in an agricultural country has normally been a rapid increase of population, due to a fall in the death-rate, accentuated, to a greater or less degree, by a rise in the birth-rate. If industry expands with extraordinary speed, it may absorb the whole, or nearly the whole, increase. That, or something like it, was what occurred in Germany between 1870 and 1910.

Even in Germany, however, in spite of the astonishing pace of her economic transformation, the number, as distinct from the percentage, of workers engaged in agriculture was not diminished. In China, where industrial development must inevitably be far slower, the most that can be hoped is that some part of the annual increase in population will find employment in industry. In that case the rural population, unless checked by other causes, will grow more slowly, but it will continue to grow. The increased pressure on the land, which would have resulted from the same proportion of the rising generation as at present—assuming that it had lived—seeking employment in agriculture, will be somewhat mitigated; but the actual pressure, which exists at present to an appalling degree, will not be diminished.

Industrialisation, therefore, like emigration, however desirable in itself, is not a substitute for the control of population through the restriction of the birth-rate. It is true, no doubt, that to contrast the former with the latter, as a temporary palliative with a fundamental remedy, is to over-simplify the problem. Palliatives offer a breathing-space which gives remedies their chance; remedies are not likely to be applied if palliatives are neglected. The effect of an increase in the output of wealth is qualitative, as well as quantitative. It not only adds to income, but alters habits; and one form which the changed habits assume is a higher standard of life, which ultimately reduces the birth-rate. The decline of the latter is a phenomenon which, as far as recent history is concerned, has

been specially characteristic of industrial societies, and for
which the environment created by an industrial civilisation
has been primarily responsible.

It is a phenomenon, however, which has hitherto appeared,
not in the early stages of industrialisation, but only when it has
run its course for some two generations. There has been a
time-lag, in short, between the fall of the death-rate, due to
increased resources, sanitation and medical care, and the fall
of the birth-rate, due to the diffusion of education, the circu-
lation of ideas, the alteration of canons of personal conduct,
and the crystallisation of economic standards at a higher level.
In the interval between the first change and the second, the
rate of growth of population has commonly increased. Whether
in European countries, in most of which, at the beginning of
last century, population was small in relation to resources,
prosperity would have been greater had that increase been
less, is a problem on which opinions differ. In China, where
the population is already excessive, and where the danger of a
capitalism based on the exploitation of cheap labour is not
remote, a similar question admits of only one answer. The
desirability, on economic grounds, of substituting the deliberate
restriction of births for the removal of part of the surplus by
death is not open to question.

If fresh waves of population do not sweep away the gains,
the modernisation of industry makes possible a higher standard
of life. Whether, and in what degree, the possibility becomes a
reality for the mass of ordinary people depends, not merely on
how much is produced, but on the terms on which it is produced, and on the manner in which it is used. It is a question,
in short, not only of technology, but of social organisation and
policy.

It is inevitable, no doubt, in a country where the burden
imposed on man by the environment is as crushing as it is in
parts of China, that machinery and power should be hailed as
the beneficent genii who will lift the load, without human
intervention being required to control their proceedings. There
is enough truth in that attitude to make dangerous its illusions.

Genii are good servants but bad masters. If the machine can emancipate, it can also enslave.

It is a question of circumstances, and of the policy appropriate to them. Given large natural resources, a population mobile, adaptable and, above all, small, and the alternative to industrial employment offered by free land, the transition from the cottage to the factory may be swift and frictionless, and the harassed farmer of yesterday undergo a painless sublimation into the car-owning, cinema-haunting mechanic of to-day. In a densely populated country, with a long habit of poverty, no general diffusion of education, little accessible spare land, and administrative services still in their infancy, the first effects of industrialisation are likely, if experience may be trusted, to be somewhat more speckled. They will be what, in the opening phases of the Industrial Revolution, they were in most regions of the West, and what in parts of China they already are—the exploitation of child labour; a working day of twelve to fifteen hours, in which the pace is set, not by the customary routine of handicraft industry, but by the speed of the machine; night work, not only for adults but for children; a shocking accident roll; a new discipline of production which is resented as an interference with personal liberty; a deterioration of the environment which goes some way to counterbalance the rise in money wages; and the existence of some employers who protest that the world will end if these conditions are altered, while the more enlightened firms, which do not regard efficiency as another name for cheating their employees, find it difficult, however good their intentions, to maintain civilised standards in the teeth of the competition of those who do.

Whether, even so, urban poverty may not be preferable to the life of many villages in China, is a matter of opinion. To that of some of them—since one cannot easily do worse than die of hunger—it certainly is; to that of others, it may be suspected, it is not. But the fact that peasants are starving in Shansi or Kansu is not a reason why factory operatives should be sweated in Shanghai or Tientsin. It is difficult to be patient

with the casuists who plead in one breath for the industrialisation of China, on the ground that it will raise the standards
of life in agriculture, and in the next defend low standards in
industry, on the ground that those prevalent in agriculture are
even lower. In reality, of course, arguments for and against
industrialisation are twenty years out of date. As the figures
show, the thing already exists. Its style and spirit in China
will not be those of the West; but, in one form or another,
it is inevitable. If it did not grow in China from within, it
would be forced on her from without, as, in considerable
measure, it already has been. The question is not whether it
shall develop, which it obviously will, but what methods it
shall use and what results it shall produce. The practical
problem is to secure its economic benefits, while avoiding, as
far as possible, its social disadvantages.

They are largely avoidable. Whether, in fact, they will be
avoided is another question. In a country where nearly three-
quarters of the population consists of peasant farmers, the new
stresses produced by the Industrial Revolution are of less
general significance, no doubt, than the evils which from time
immemorial have haunted the village. They are already, however, sufficiently acute. With the development of manufactures,
their gravity will increase.

The issues which arise are of three main kinds. They relate
to the planning and organisation of production, to the standards of employment in factory industry, and to the conditions
of life created by the growth of urbanisation. At present, in
spite of much valuable work done by Chinese students, opinion,
even in responsible quarters, appears to be imperfectly informed as to the dangers which exist and the possibility of
averting them. Public announcements[1] encourage the hope
that the error of allowing the basic industries of the future,

[1] See, e.g., the programme for the development of the iron and steel, electrical,
machine-making and certain other industries, laid by Dr. K'ung before the fifth
plenary session of the Central Executive Committee, March, 1929 (Tyau, *Two
Years of Nationalist China*, pp. 205–206); Dr. K'ung's address to the Conference on
the People's Livelihood, Shanghai, February 22, 1931; and the programme of
industrial reconstruction laid before the National People's Convention in May,
1931 (see *China's Ten Years' Plan* in *Pacific Affairs*, September 1931).

other than agriculture, to be exploited with a single eye to commercial profit, may be avoided by China; but, though principles have been stated, the precise method of applying them remains to be determined. While the traditional organisation of handicraft industry is obviously, in parts of the country, breaking up, there are few signs that clear views have been formed of the part which such crafts are to play in the future economy of China—whether, for example, their decline is to be accepted, on the English precedent, as desirable and inevitable, or whether, as in Germany, an attempt is to be made to preserve certain among them, by improving their productive technique and business organisation. The effect of urbanisation on health, the family system, traditional standards of conduct and social sanctions, and the nature of the agencies which may offer, as the latter decay, a substitute for them, still awaits investigation. The hope for the future is that the conditions of life of the worker on the land may indirectly be raised by the influence of the higher standard which should be possible for workers in manufactures based on power-driven machinery. The danger is that the standard of life of the worker in manufacturing industry may be depressed to the level of that obtaining on the land.

The first point which calls for consideration is one which has received less attention than it deserves. It is the possibility of improving the methods of handicraft and domestic industries. It is a mistake to acquiesce in the common assumption that, because mass production is the condition of efficiency in certain important branches of enterprise, it is therefore equally desirable in all, and that to accelerate its introduction is the only possible method of promoting economic progress. That blunder was made in many parts of Europe, and is now, in some of them, being partially corrected. It should be avoided in China. She is, and will long continue to be, overwhelmingly a country of peasants and handicraftsmen. To ignore the possibilities of her traditional economic system would be a grave error of judgment. The course of wisdom, as Professor Tayler has urged, is to aid these small producers to maintain their position, by assisting them to improve their technique and to strengthen the financial and commercial organisation of their industries. Much work on these lines has been done in the last twenty years in certain European countries. The National Economic Council recently established at Nanking should examine the methods employed, and consider by what means they can be applied in China. The measures required would naturally include the dissemination of the knowledge of the best processes by education and propaganda, and the organisation of co-operative societies for credit, marketing and the purchase of raw materials.

Whatever steps, however, may be taken with that object, an extension of mass production is probably inevitable. It is natural, therefore, that the conditions of employment in factory industry, and, in particular, in the larger factories, the majority of which are of recent growth, should be among the problems which have aroused most interest. The absence of recognised standards, such as are established by trade unions—in itself a great evil—make generalisation precarious. Much the most important factory city in China is Shanghai, with 222,681 factory workers, followed, at a long distance, by Wusih, with 48,875, Tientsin with 36,634, and Hankow with 9,720. Much the largest single factory industry is cotton-spinning, with 252,032 workers in China as a whole, and 94,342 in Shanghai, 16,798 in Tientsin, 15,780 in Wusih and 1,951 in Hankow. While some excellent work has been done on wages in China, notably by Professor Franklin Ho, Professor Fong, Dr. D. K. Lieu and Dr. Tao, comprehensive and reliable statistics are still scanty, and figures as to earnings must be taken with reservations. With that caution, it may be stated that in Shanghai the highest earnings per day of adult male cotton spinners were reported in 1930 by the Bureau of Social Affairs to be $1.68 (Mex.) and the lowest to be $0.40, the average earnings per month being $15.57,[1] and that in Wusih their

---

[1] Fang Fu-an, *Chinese Labour: An Economic and Statistical Survey* (Shanghai, 1931), p. 47, quoting from *Shanghai Industry* (Chinese), ed. Bureau of Social Affairs of the Municipality of Greater Shanghai.

average daily earnings were reported by Dr. D. K. Lieu in 1929 to be $0.40 to $0.50, in Tientsin $0.40, and in Hankow from $0.36 to $0.65.[1] Figures as to hours are less unreliable. In Shanghai, the maximum (and usual) hours in cotton mills were reported in 1930 to be twelve, the minimum ten and a half. In Wusih, Tientsin and Hankow a twelve-hour day in cotton mills is said to be almost universal,[2] children working the same hours as adults. It is stated that a night-shift of twelve hours, with the exception of a few mills, is the general rule, and the working week normally consists of seven days.[3]

There is no reason to suppose that conditions in cotton mills are worse than those obtaining in other factories. On the contrary, such evidence as exists suggests that they are better. Since, with a few exceptions, the firms in question work a twelve-hour shift, and employ children at night, they seem, it is true, to have little to boast of. As usual, however, it is not in these large concerns, but in the smaller factories which are much more numerous, and which employ in the aggregate a far larger body of workers, that exploitation is seen at its worst. Their standards of employment, if they can be said to have standards at all, resemble those customary in many handicraft industries. When machinery and power are introduced, the dirt, overcrowding, overheating, absence of sanitation, and long hours, which are traditional in some, though by no means in all, of the latter, remain unaltered. The difference is that discipline becomes more rigid, dependence on child labour more general, risks of accident greater, and the pressure on the workers more intense. But the difference is fundamental. The attempt sometimes made in China to-day, as in the England of the early nineteenth century, to palliate the conditions of factory industry on the ground that those who suffer from them are accustomed to nothing better, is, apart from all questions of humanity, singularly lacking in intelligence. The contrast is that between an untidy home and an ill-

[1] *Problems of the Pacific*, 1929 (University of Chicago Press, 1930), p. 262.

[2] Fang Fu-an, *op. cit.*, pp. 34–37.

[3] For figures of earnings and hours based on the Report of 1930, see Table VI in the Appendix.

conducted prison. The easy-going employer, who has worked with his men like a father with his family, is replaced by a tyrannical foreman, whose position depends on the output he gets. The pace is set, not by the older workmen, who know the craft, but by the machine. The casual, half-domestic atmosphere of the old-fashioned workshop, with its gossip, smoking, breaks to run to the door to chat with a passer-by or take sides in a street quarrel, meals shared by workmen and master, and endlessly circulating tea, gives way to factory routine, without the factory standards in the matter of leisure, safety, sanitation and working rules, which alone make it tolerable. The attractions, in short, of small-scale industry disappear, but its defects are exaggerated.

Professor Fong,[1] in a valuable study of industrialisation in Hopei, has described in detail the evils which have accompanied it in Tientsin and the neighbourhood. Machinery in cotton mills, flour mills, soda factories, salt refineries and other establishments is commonly unfenced, and, though no reliable statistics are available, the rate of accidents is reported to be high. The incidence of industrial disease is heavy. Juvenile labour tends to encroach on that of adults; of 47,519 workers in Tientsin factories, 9,730, or no less than one-fifth, were, at the time when the inquiry was made, under sixteen years of age. "In respect of the hours of work," Professor Fong remarks, "the factory workers in Hopei have not as yet participated in the benefits resulting from industrialisation." Hours in Tientsin factories appear to average 12·74 per day; in match factories they vary from 10 to 14; in hosiery knitting, carpet weaving, and rayon and cotton weaving, they average 11·1 per day; in flour mills two shifts are worked, of 12 hours each.

What is even more surprising, the higher level of pecuniary earnings, which machine industry, whatever its other disadvantages, is commonly thought to offer, appears not to be attained by factory operatives in Tientsin. "The workers in modern industries," to quote the words of Dr. Fong, "do not

[1] *Industrialisation in Hopei, with Special Reference to Tientsin,* by H. D. Fong (Nankai University Committee on Social and Economic Research, 1930).

seem to share the increment due to increased productivity."
The average wage per day for ten types of crafts—carpenters,
masons, stone-cutters, bricklayers, roof-layers, plumbers, glass-
cutters, tailors, painters and shoe-makers—amounted to 69.7
cents in 1927, 66.4 cents in 1928, 68.8 cents in 1929; while
that for eleven types of factory workers—electricians, printers,
cotton workers (male and female), matchmakers (male and
female), cigarette makers (male and female), flour-mill
workers, leather workers, and bone-powder grinders—
amounted to 39.8 cents in 1927, 37.8 cents in 1928, 47.6 cents
in 1929. The average earnings of factory operatives are reduced,
of course, by the inclusion of women in three of these occupations. So marked a difference between their wages and those of
handicraft workers remains, nevertheless, somewhat surprising.[1]

It would obviously be impossible, without prolonged investigation, to determine how far these facts are typical of those to be
found in other industrial centres. If conclusions may be drawn
from the inquiries hitherto carried out, it would seem reasonable to say that, with the exception of certain individual
establishments, which have pursued a more intelligent policy,
the conditions generally obtaining in factory employment
recall those of the first, and worst, phase of the Industrial
Revolution in England. Not only are hours preposterously
long, and wages almost incredibly low, but part of the work is
often done by relays of cheap or unpaid juvenile workers,
sometimes imported from the country, and occasionally, it is
alleged, actually sold to their employers, in shops which are
frequently little better than barns, and in which the most
elementary conditions of health and safety appear to be
ignored. It is possible, in certain cities, to go through a succession of these little establishments, which may or may not be
technically factories, largely staffed with boys between eight and
sixteen years of age, working twelve to fourteen hours per day
for seven days in the week, and sleeping at night on the floor

[1] It should be noted, however, that the wages of handicraft and factory workers
are not in all cases comparable, owing to the fact that (i) in some cases the
former are provided with board and lodging by their employers; (ii) the wages
fixed by the gilds for the former sometimes include certain overhead expenses.

of the shop, in which the lighting is such as to make it certain that the sight of many of them will be permanently injured, machinery is completely unguarded, the air is loaded with poisonous dust, which there is no ventilation to remove, and the buildings are unprovided, in spite of municipal by-laws, with emergency exits, with the result that, in the event of fire, some proportion of the workers will almost certainly be burned. Manufactures conducted under these conditions, most of which are unnecessary, and which are not only injurious to the workers but a serious obstacle to efficient production, are—to speak with moderation—of questionable advantage. Those who play with edged tools, without knowing how to handle them, will cut their fingers, if they do not, in addition, cut their neighbours' throats. To import western industrial technique without importing western methods of controlling it is to prepare a disaster.

The appropriate agencies for controlling it are the same in China as in other countries. They are trade unionism and industrial legislation. No trade union movement, as distinct from a gild system embracing both masters and journeymen, appears to have existed in China till twelve years ago. Starting in or about 1919, it experienced the repression by the criminal law which in most countries has accompanied the first phase of its growth. It expanded rapidly in the atmosphere created by the militant nationalism of 1923–1927, was then found an embarrassing ally by those whom it had helped to carry to success, and was, accordingly, reorganised by the Government, with the object of purging it of influences regarded by the latter as undesirable.

In June, 1928, legislation[1] was promulgated which made provision for conciliation and arbitration in industrial disputes. The machinery can be set in motion on the application of either party, and a strike or lock-out is illegal during the continuance of the proceedings. A Trade Union Act was promulgated in October, 1929, and enforced as from November of that year, which determines the legal status of unions. While recognising the right of association, it surrounds it

[1] Amended March 17, 1930. I have used the English version of this and the following Acts, printed in Fang Fu-an, *Chinese Labour* (Appendix).

with restrictions which appear to a western observer to deprive
it of much of its value. A union, as a condition of enjoying
such protection as the law offers, must lodge an application for
registration with the proper authority, which may either grant
or refuse it.[1] No conclusion, revision or cancellation of an
agreement ("collective contract") between a union and employer or employers is valid unless approved by the proper
authority.[2] No interference, a highly ambiguous word, with
the work of non-unionists is permitted.[3] No strike shall be
declared unless (a) attempts have been made to settle the
dispute by conciliation and arbitration, and (b) "the case has
subsequently been referred to a general meeting of the Union,
at which at least two-thirds of its members have voted by
secret ballot in favour of the strike."[4] It seems clear that, if
such rules are enforced in practice, no union disapproved of by
the political authorities of the day can come into existence, and
no union which exists can make agreements other than those
which such authorities approve.[5]

Trade unionism had its origin, in most western countries, in
the activities of small clubs of highly skilled craftsmen, with a
long tradition of organisation, who found themselves threatened by machinery and cheap juvenile labour. In China, while
there are numerous cases of a union springing from a gild, the
backbone of the movement has consisted of the workers in the
newer industries. Statistics of trade union membership have
from time to time been published. At the height of the boom
of 1927, it was put at 3,065,000; in 1928 the Ministry of
Industry, Commerce and Labour reported 999 unions, with
1,860,030 members; and the report of 1930 states that there
were in that year, in twenty-six cities, 741 unions, with 574,766

[1] Act as to Labour Unions, Chap. I, Arts. 4 and 5. "The proper administrative
and supervisory authority" is defined as "the Provincial Government and the
authorities of the District (*Hsien*) and Municipality (*Shih*) where the union is
located."
[2] Chap. II, Art. 15 (1).   [3] Chap. III, Art. 20.   [4] Chap. III, Art. 23.
[5] The Ministry of Industry, Commerce and Labour reported that 200 trade
unions in Kwangtung, and 2,802 branch unions with 494,819 members in Hopei,
had been dissolved in 1928 (*Labour Unions in Various Places*, Appendix, pp. 7–31).
On the general situation, see Fang Fu-an, *Chinese Labour*; H. D. Fong, *China's
Industrialisation*; and L. K. Tao and S. H. Lin, *op. cit.*

members. What is of greater importance is the number of trade unionists in the large industrial centres. It was given, for that year, at 107,186 in Canton, 68,133 in Shanghai, 52,625 in Hankow, 45,186 in Swantu, and 34,906 in Hangchow. Of the total number, 23 per cent were stated to be employed in the textile industries, 18 per cent in transport, 14 per cent in machine making, 10 per cent in the industries concerned with the preparation of food, and 7 per cent in the chemical industry. Owing to the lack of an occupational census, it is impossible to state what percentage of workers in different industries is organised. It is obviously, however, extremely low.

For a country where capitalist industry is as young as in China, trade unionism has made, if these figures can be trusted, considerable progress. The figure of 574,766 trade unionists in twenty-six cities in 1930 is higher than the corresponding figure usually given for either France or Germany in the nineties of last century. The difficulty is to know its exact significance. Trade union membership is not so simple a conception as at first sight appears; a membership figure means one thing when it is based on records of fully paid-up members, and quite another when it represents merely a guess by officials. A more serious gap in the literature is the lack of any adequate account of the constitution, organisation and activities of such unions as exist. Sketches of the external aspects of the movement—its growth and past political affiliations—have appeared in abundance. But nothing is easier, in some countries, than to organise unions which exist on paper, and which, apart from providing a living for their officers, do nothing in particular. What is required, before any judgment can be formed of the real significance of trade unionism in China, is work by Chinese economists of a much more intensive and systematic kind than appears yet to have been undertaken. It is an account of the machinery and procedure of collective bargaining, of the area of industry governed by agreements between employers and trade unions, and of the extent to which such agreements, when made, are observed in practice.

In the absence of evidence on these essential points, any

decided opinion as to the practical achievements and probable future of trade unionism in China is clearly impossible. The impression—possibly the mistaken impression—of a superficial observer is that, while its growth has been remarkable, it suffers at present from the deficiencies which have in most countries marked the beginning of the movement. There is more effervescence than solid organisation. The workers who form its membership have as yet thrown up comparatively few leaders from their own ranks. Trade union law is not happily conceived, and trade union business is exposed to the meddlesome interference of politicians who, whatever their abilities in other directions, have no special competence for handling industrial questions. Most unions are still shop unions, dealing with isolated undertakings, and are not yet sufficiently powerful or well organised to make agreements covering a large body of employers in a considerable section of a trade. Many employers are still in the primitive stage of refusing to "recognise" the union. The result is that the establishment of tolerable conditions by the application of common rules has rarely yet been attained, and that standards in one establishment are constantly liable to be dragged down by undercutting on the part of another.

In the early days of a trade union movement such weaknesses are to be expected. It may play, in spite of them, a useful part; but to expect that it will be able in any near future to maintain the minimum standards, which are required if industry is to develop on sound lines, is obviously utopian. Either such standards will be established and enforced by public action, or they will not be enforced at all. Earlier measures for the protection of industrial workers, such as the provisional factory regulations issued by the Peiping Government in 1923, those issued by the Government in Hupeh in 1926, the provisional labour law for the north-western provinces issued by Marshall Feng Yu-hsiang in 1927, and the Peiping Government regulations of the same year, had been local in scope, and largely inoperative in practice. There was good reason for thinking, however, that the advent to power of the Nanking Government would be followed by a serious attempt to establish an industrial code such as exists in other civilised countries.

The necessity for it had been repeatedly emphasised by Chinese thinkers of unimpeachable orthodoxy. Dr. Sun Yat-sen, in his classical work, spoke with warm approval of "the use of Government power to better the working man's education and to protect his health, to improve factories and machinery so that working conditions may be perfectly safe and comfortable."[1] The manifesto of the first national congress of the Kuomintang emphasised the evils of unrestricted capitalist industrialism, and mentioned "labour laws to improve the livelihood of the labourers"[2] as being among measures which it was pledged to carry out. According to a volume produced in 1930 by Dr. Tyau, then Director of the Intelligence and Publicity Department of the Ministry of Foreign Affairs, the policy of the Government included "measures for the elevation of the workers' status," the establishment of "factory councils to facilitate consultation between the employers and the employees," and the creation of "a factory inspectorate to enforce labour laws and regulations throughout the country."[3] When therefore a Factory Law was promulgated in December, 1929,[4] it was reasonable to assume that some steps would be taken to correct evils whose gravity, so far from being denied by the authorities, had repeatedly been emphasised by them.

The law, it had been announced, was to come into operation

[1] *San Min Chu I*, trans. Frank W. Price (Shanghai, 1929), p. 386.

[2] T'ang Leang Li, *The Inner History of the Chinese Revolution*, pp. 166 *et seq.*; and M. T. Z. Tyau, *Two Years of Nationalist China*, p. 448.

[3] Tyau, *op. cit.*, pp. 207–208.

[4] Trans. by N. F. Allman and Lowe Chuan-hua (*China Weekly Review*, Shanghai). A valuable analysis of the law will be found in three articles by Miss Eleanor N. Hinder on *The New Factory Law of the Nanking Government* (*North China Daily News*, January 15, 16, 17, 1931). For an account of the developments preceding it, see Fang Fu-an, *op. cit.*; Ta Chen, *Labour in China During the Civil Wars*; and Jefferson D. H. Lamb, *The Origins and Development of Social Legislation in China*; and for the situation in 1931, H. D. Fong, *op. cit.*, and L. K. Tao and S. H. Lin, *op. cit.* The law contains various other important provisions, e.g. as to wages, contracts of employment, compensation and pensions, welfare, factory councils and apprentices, not referred to above.

on February 1, 1931.   The most important reforms contained
in it were as follows :—

i. the prohibition of the employment in factories of children
under the age of fourteen ;

ii. the prohibition of the employment of children of fourteen
to sixteen, and of women, on certain processes, for example those
involving inflammable or poisonous substances, exposure to
dust or noxious fumes, and the cleaning, oiling and repairing
of machinery in motion ;

iii. the limitation of "the regular working day" for adults to
eight hours, subject to two exceptions :

(a) that it may be fixed at ten hours, where this is necessary
    owing to special local conditions and the nature of
    the work,

(b) that it may be extended to twelve hours, provided that
    not more than thirty-six hours' overtime are worked in
    a month, that overtime is paid at the rate of time and
    a third, and that reasons for working overtime are
    presented to the "proper authority" ;

iv. the prohibition of nightwork for women and children,
for the former between 10 p.m. and 6 a.m., for the latter
between 7 p.m. and 6 a.m. ;

v. the prohibition of more than eight hours' work per day
for child workers (i.e. workers between fourteen and sixteen
years of age) ;

vi. provision as to rest (half an hour after five hours' continuous work), one day off work in seven, and annual holidays,
on a scale graduated according to the length of the worker's
service ;

vii. provisions as to safety and health, e.g. the structure of
the factory, the fencing of machinery, ventilation, lighting,
and sanitary conditions ;

viii. provisions as to welfare : e.g. employers are to provide
ten hours' education per week for child workers, and are to
give leave with full wages to women workers before and after
childbirth for a period of eight weeks in all.

The law also lays down rules of great importance as to wages and the termination of contracts of employment. As the date at which it was to come into operation approached, agitation was directed against it, and its application was accordingly postponed for six months. It came into force on August 1, 1931.

The case for industrial legislation has been much debated in China, but the discussion has not always been according to knowledge. The considerations which arise are partly general, partly special. The latter relate to the economic and administrative arrangements obtaining in a particular place at a particular moment; on the former, the experience of other countries, which have faced similar problems in the past, suggests certain conclusions. The first is that the task which, in the first instance, is most important, is not to fix a high minimum, but to fix *some* minimum, which later can be raised, and to enforce it when fixed. The second is that the practicability of enforcing compliance with the law does not depend merely on the content of the obligations which it imposes, but on due notice being given of them, and on sufficient time being allowed for the necessary adjustments in industrial organisation to be made. The third is that, provided that this condition is observed, the fear that industry will be injured by legal regulation is commonly exaggerated. These apprehensions have always been aroused, and not unnaturally aroused, on occasions when legislation is first introduced. It has usually been found, however, that, if the necessary time were accorded, the ability of producers to adapt themselves and their undertakings to the new conditions created by the law was greater than they themselves at first supposed. Both legislators and manufacturers must consider, in short, the possibilities, not merely of the moment, but of the next ten years. The former must not discredit the principle of industrial legislation by pitching its requirements so high as to provoke a reaction. The latter must recognise that industrial organisation is not fixed and unalterable, but susceptible of modifications, and that these modifications make possible standards that, at first sight, seem impracticable.

The special difficulties confronting the enforcement of an industrial code in China are not open to dispute. Her machine industries are still young. Certain among them have to face keen foreign competition in the home market. High interest rates make overhead charges abnormally heavy. The workers are still largely untrained, and unaccustomed to the discipline of factory life; some of them, indeed, even while working in factories, remain villagers temporarily transplanted to towns. The majority of establishments are small, and not easily subjected to strict supervision. A competent factory inspectorate, with the necessary experience and technique, still has to be created.

These difficulties, it is true, are not so peculiar to China as is sometimes suggested. They have been experienced, at one time or another, by most industrial countries. France and Germany developed their manufactures in the teeth of the competition of British producers, equipped with larger capital and a more efficient technique; the personnel of the new factories was almost everywhere recruited from an agricultural population, unhabituated to the speed and intensity of machine production; the early factories of Europe, like those of China, were little more than small workshops. If the existence of such conditions had been permitted to prevent the passage of factory legislation, no factory legislation would ever have been passed. It is proper, nevertheless, that Chinese social policy should take account of the stage of development reached by Chinese industry, and that industrial legislation should begin, not at the point which, after a century of struggle, it has reached in the West, but at one more nearly resembling that at which it there began, though, of course, as far in advance of the latter as is practicable. It is reasonable that it should advance experimentally and by degrees, and, while providing for the strict enforcement of such minimum as it prescribes, should take account, in determining it, of the fact that in the past no minimum has existed.

It is one thing, however, to recognise that standards fixed may at first have to be modest; it is quite another to acquiesce in the absence of any standards at all, or in the indefinite continuance of standards as low as may alone in the first instance be capable of enforcement. Industrial legislation, it must be remembered, is not a matter which can be settled once for all by a single enactment; it ought to be susceptible of continuous improvement. If that view of the matter is correct, the practical conclusion to be drawn from it is that the course of wisdom is to accept the fact that the conditions aimed at must be established by successive stages, rather than, by attempting to establish them at one stroke, to fail to establish them effectively at all. This does not mean that—to give only two examples—the sound ideal of an eight-hour day and of the prohibition of the labour of children under fourteen, should be abandoned, or its realisation relegated to an indefinite future. What it does mean is that legislation should provide for the immediate reduction of hours to ten and for their subsequent reduction, after an interval of years fixed in the Act itself, first to nine, and then to eight; for the immediate prohibition of the labour of children under twelve; and for the prohibition later, after an interval similarly fixed, of the labour of children under fourteen.

If that policy is pursued, the better standards come automatically into operation, unless the original Act is repealed or amended. But time is given for the necessary readjustments to be made, and the danger that the law will remain inoperative in practice is mitigated. Nor must it be forgotten that the enforcement of legislation depends on the development of a skilled inspectorate. The objection to factory legislation in general on the ground that no such inspectorate at present exists is clearly invalid, for the necessary administrative service is not likely to be created until a body of law exists for it to administer. It is true, however, that the serious business of protecting the worker only begins when the Act comes into operation, and that the duty of making certain that he enjoys in fact the rights conferred on him by law devolves on the inspectors. The administration of factory legislation, as distinct from its mere enactment, is a technical, and, as regards certain sides of the subject, a highly technical matter. It is important that a high standard of efficiency should be set at the start, and that the code which the inspectors are called upon to enforce should be one that is enforceable.

If, however, experience suggests the wisdom of proceeding by successive stages, its lessons as to the importance of establishing standards at the highest level possible, and of continuously raising them, are even more emphatic. The extinct superstitions of the West enjoy a hale and tranquil old age in parts of the East. The visitor is still sometimes confronted with the plain man's argument—and plain men in China are even plainer than elsewhere—that the demand for the strict regulation by law of child labour, hours, wages and working conditions is the expression of an amiable, but impracticable, humanitarianism, which ignores the stern realities of business life. So he is driven, in spite of himself, to labour platitudes. He is compelled to point out that, so far from factory legislation being injurious to industry, its effect is to divert competition from the deterioration of standards of employment into the introduction of better methods of organisation and production, and to protect the more efficient and enlightened manufacturers, who already normally offer better conditions than those legally required, from being undersold by their less competent or less scrupulous rivals.

It is arguable, no doubt, that it is a mistake to desire to see the extension in China of large-scale industry, based on machinery and power. Those who adopt that attitude may reasonably object to factory legislation. If, however, as seems more commonly to be held by Chinese thinkers, it is important that modern methods of manufacture should be adopted as rapidly and as widely as possible, there is no reasonable doubt that legislation establishing minimum standards of employment, which compels producers to modernise their technique and overhaul their organisation, tends to accelerate their introduction. Nor is it a matter of minor significance that, in the absence of such standards, a working personnel of the calibre required to make possible the transition to a more efficient economic system will not be available.

Modern industry requires not merely modern machinery, but the modern engineer, modern factory operative and modern miner. They will certainly not be recruited from a population pitched into industry at the age of eight or nine, worked eleven to fourteen hours a day except when it is unemployed, decimated by preventable disease, unable to read or write, paid a wage insufficient to maintain it in physical health, and sunk in a condition of mental apathy, broken by occasional fits of violent exasperation. If Chinese opinion, in short, is serious in desiring to accelerate an expansion of manufacturing industry, it must devote as much attention to developing the human resources of the country as to improving its mechanical equipment and economic organisation. It must insist that standards of employment shall be fixed and enforced, not on any plane of impracticable excellence, but at the highest level which undertakings conducted with reasonable efficiency can at any given moment attain, and shall periodically be raised.

CHAPTER VI

POLITICS AND EDUCATION

It is easy to suggest methods by which, in the course of the next half-century, China could improve her agricultural and industrial organisation. What is technically feasible, however, may be politically impracticable, and the question whether the conditions of public life permit the necessary steps to be taken raises different issues. To forecast the future is impossible. The country is so vast; the interests involved so various and complex; the absence of the settled forms and habits of political procedure, which canalise action elsewhere, so conducive to abrupt deviations and unpredictable changes; the uncertainties caused by foreign intervention so multitudinous and distracting.

Political forces in China resemble Chinese rivers. The pressure on the dykes is enormous, but unseen; it is only when they burst that the strain is realised. The visitor, who sees only the externals, inevitably miscalculates the force of the current. Nor, when he turns for instruction to foreign residents in China and to his Chinese acquaintances, can he always be certain of receiving enlightenment. Both are apt to be more interested in the problems arising from contacts between China and foreign nations than in those of China herself. The former may have investigated the economic and social life of the interior of the country, which is not that of the ports; but, unless they have done so, their opinion on Chinese politics is not necessarily more authoritative than is that of Kensington on the conditions of the Durham coal-field or the Lancashire cotton industry. The latter are not infrequently too exasperated by the weakness of China in the face of foreign Powers to be disposed to consider the internal circumstances to which, in part, it is due.

Their attitude is natural; but mere indignation is futile and undignified. The Treaty of 1922, by which it was intended to secure China against the recurrence of foreign aggression, has now, in effect, been torn up by Japan.[1] What action the League will find it possible to take, it is still too early to say. It is intelligible, at any rate, that some Chinese should feel that the moral for China is that she will obtain consideration from foreign nations when she is able to demand it, and not before. She will be able to demand it when she has succeeded in creating a unified state, with an effective central government, commanding the unquestioned allegiance of the majority of Chinese, and supported by the resources which only a generation of economic progress can provide. In building such a state, she will make use, if she is wise, of the technical skill and administrative experience which the West can supply. But, to create the environment in which alone they can function, she must rely on herself.

It is to that task, not to sterile, if well-founded, denunciations of western and Japanese Imperialism, that the brains and energy of young China should be turned. Unequal treaties, extra-territoriality, concessions, the Manchurian question—these matters, if China succeeds in setting her own house in order, will settle themselves. Unless she does so, they will not be settled at all. The right motto in regard to them for the rising generation of Chinese is *pensons-y toujours, n'en parlons jamais*. If they are to make their country count abroad, they must first strengthen it at home. They must create a stable and unified political system, in the absence of which it is idle to

[1] In Article I of the Treaty of February 16, 1922, the nine signatory Powers (the United States, Belgium, the British Empire, France, Italy, Japan, Holland, Portugal and China) bound themselves:

"To respect the sovereignty, the independence and the territorial and administrative integrity of China; to provide the fullest and most unembarrassed opportunity to China to develop and maintain for herself an effective and stable government; to use their influence for the purpose of maintaining the principle of equal opportunity for the commerce and industry of all nations throughout the territory of China; and to refrain from taking advantage of conditions in China in order to seek special rights or privileges which would abridge the rights of subjects or citizens of friendly states and from countenancing action inimical to the security of such states." Further, they agreed that "there should be full and frank communication between the Contracting Powers concerned, whenever a situation arose which involved the application of the Treaty in the opinion of any one of them."

talk either of national independence or of economic reconstruction.

It is notorious that such a system does not exist to-day. The first problem of Chinese politics is vast and fundamental. It is not who shall govern the state, but whether there shall be a state at all. It is whether public power shall exist. China has known no Roman Empire. The idea of a sovereign; of an even pressure of law; of the impersonal majesty of an authority to which, and not to his family and his friends, the individual owes allegiance; of the *Res publica*, which men remembered dimly in Europe when all else had slipped, and struggled back to, as to a rock—that idea is not an ancient part of the nation's mental furniture, but a modern growth, which strives breathlessly for life amid interests and sentiments sprung from a different world, that overshadow and stifle it. The thought of China, one and indivisible, is no doubt a power; but it is primarily the reflection of a great cultural tradition. As a political force, expressed in the working routine of habits and institutions, it still has to be created.

The reason is historical. Societies develop only the aptitudes which they need. China did not evolve a highly organised political system, because, until recently, she did not require one. Isolated by geography, and with a singularly homogeneous civilisation in the vast range of her territory, she experienced, till little more than a century ago, neither the external pressure which in Europe shaped the state, nor the rivalry of numerous independent centres of energy, which was a principal stimulus to economic progress. Western observers are shocked by her political incoherence, and some aspects of it are shocking. They do not always remember, however, the natural facts of which it is the consequence. In population, area and diversity of economic conditions, China is to be compared, not with a single European nation, but with Europe as a whole. But the geographical and historical conditions which have caused Europe to be organised in over a score of national states have, for good or evil, been absent from China. Not only, if population be the test, is she the largest nation in the world, but she has possessed for a longer period than any other some of the essential characteristics of a single organism. Hence problems, which in the West are international, are in China domestic; breakdowns, which in the former result in wars between states, in the latter take the form of civil disorder. Which produce most misery it is difficult to say.

China is an organism, however, of a peculiar kind, which has no modern western analogy. Her unity, like that of mediaeval Christendom, has been the unity of a civilisation rather than of a political system. Like Christendom, she was conscious that she was not merely a state, but the embodiment of a spirit—an oasis of culture and light, divided, as by a wall, from the surging barbarism of the outer darkness which beat against her borders—and, as in Christendom, the unity which she derived from an ideal did not preclude the occurrence of violent internal struggles. It rested on the Chinese family, uniting, not the living alone, but the living, the dead and those yet to be born, in an undying community; on the stable, patient routine of the Chinese village; on the common heritage of a philosophy which made personal relations, and the conduct appropriate to them, not metaphysics or political obligations, the foundation of its scheme; on a tradition and style of behaviour which turned each individual into the expression of a whole people, and to perpetuate which in himself and his descendants was happiness and virtue; on a common sense of the insignificance of the present in the great ocean of the past, which even to-day causes many Chinese to think in centuries where the West thinks in decades. Custom, not law, fixed the framework of existence; ethics, not theology or political interests, gave life its meaning. Till the close of the last century, government consisted of little more than the preservation of order and the extraction of taxes by imperial officials, with such additions as were needed to provide emoluments for themselves, subject to the check of rebellion when conventional claims were exceeded. Thus, instead of advancing on all fronts at once, China was at the same time both mature and retarded. She had the excellences and defects of a non-political society. The private virtues flourished; the public were atrophied. Precocious in culture, she did not grow the hard shell of material organisation, which protects, and sometimes stifles, it. Her intellectual and aesthetic achievements were on one plane; her political and economic system remained on another.

Such a society could survive in isolation. In the nineteenth century the fragile vase crashed against brazen vessels. Once more the barbarian broke in, this time from the south. The traditional order collapsed, not merely, as in the past, in an anarchic interregnum between rival dynasties, but in principle and essence. Its effects, however, remained, for they were wrought into the very texture of Chinese life. When, therefore, the long agony of the old régime finally ended in 1911, the problem confronting the Revolution was immensely more difficult than had been faced by the western movements which it took as its model. It was, not merely to capture political power, for such power did not exist; it was to create it. It was to establish the authority of the Central Government in a society in which government, in the western sense of the term, had hitherto been unknown. It was to unify a country larger than Europe, in which neither the material conditions of unity, in the shape of communications, nor its psychological foundations, were yet in being. And it was to do all this at a moment when the subtle sanctions of the past were dissolving in the acid of western science, when the social system of a thousand years was being increasingly dislocated by new economic strains, and when the foreigner was watching his chance to fish in troubled waters, as, anticipating 1931, Japan, a consistent imperialist, who had improved on her teachers, did in 1915.

History gave little help. The French Revolution had inherited—to mention nothing else—roads and a centralised bureaucracy; the Russian was to inherit railways and a police system. China possessed neither; her legacy from the past was culture, and, if not chaos, an absence of governmental machinery which made chaos not remote. Faced with the new forces which broke on her from the West, her situation was what that of Europe might have been, had she stepped, without an intervening period of preparation, from the fifteenth century to the twentieth. The knowledge needed to cope with it was sought in the countries whence the shock had come. The effects of the New Learning were profound; but its light sometimes dazzled and bewildered, as well as illuminated. The Revolution had been made by the first generation of students to receive a western education. They had learned more, however, in the Japanese and American universities, where most of them received it, of western technique than of western social organisation, and more of both than of the Chinese realities to which the lessons had to be applied. To lift the load of the past, China required, not merely new technical devices and new political forms, but new conceptions of law, administration and political obligations, and new standards of conduct in governments, administrators, and the society which produced them. The former could be, and were, borrowed. The latter had to be grown. One scheme of life, long accepted without question, had lost its prestige; its successor was too immature to occupy the vacant throne. The result was an interregnum. It was an interval of confusion, in which everything seemed possible and nothing certain.

Most societies have undergone, in one form or another, an analogous experience. In China, owing partly to her mere size, partly to the physical difficulties of communication, partly to the absence of a general system of education, which results in the isolation of the westernised intelligentsia from the mass of the population, partly to the depth of the chasm dividing two types of thought and culture, it cannot but be protracted. Its result is the divergence between principles and practice, programmes and performance, words and acts, which at first perplexes even a visitor long accustomed to such contrasts.

He is interested in some particular problem or line of policy. He is shown a scheme of reform more complete than any which will be applied in his own country in the next quarter of a century. He pricks up his ears, and inquires what is being done to carry it out. He learns that nothing is being done, that no one is very sanguine that anything will be done, that there is little of the finance or trained administrative *personnel* required to do it, that the last official concerned in the business was not wholly above suspicion in the matter of money, and that his successor cannot visit the areas which most need attention for fear of being kidnapped. He hears much of China united under the Nationalist Government. Then he takes a map, goes through the provinces one by one, marks with a pencil those where the authority of Nanking is effective, those where it is nominal, those where it is openly defied. His perspective changes. The capital dwindles to a city effectively governing, perhaps, six or seven provinces out of thirty, in a continent partly friendly, partly indifferent, partly hostile. It is France in the twelfth century, on a scale immensely greater—Paris and the Ile de France, a little circle of light, in one corner, and, for the rest, a welter of liberties. Having first rationalised too much, he next, unless he is more than commonly self-restrained, throws reason to the winds. He began by trying to find in the politics of China an eastern variant of those of London or Paris. He ends sometimes by exclaiming that the thing is meaningless, and that there are no politics in China, or that what politics there are serve only as the drapery of a primitive struggle for money and power between rival dynasts.

The modern state in the West was not made in a generation. The European who derides the failure of China to build in thirty years a level highway from the old world to the new must have read to little purpose the tragic history of his own continent. To suppose that China is unique in her political disorders is an illusion. They are the characteristic, not of a country, but of a phase of civilisation, from which other societies have painfully emerged, but from which, owing, first, to her long isolation, and, next, to its abrupt termination, China is only now emerging. Civil war; banditry; the unorganised feudalism of military commanders, who raise private armies, grind the peasants with private taxes, and wage, when they fall out, private wars; the nepotism and jobbery produced by the doctrine that the first duty of the individual is to provide for his relations, and that it is permissible for that purpose to rob the state; the absence of public spirit, of a solidarity extending beyond the circle of the family, which permits sick men to die in the streets and murders to go unreported—such phenomena were as common in the Europe of the past as in the China of to-day.

In a world economically one, however, a community which goes its own pace cannot avoid being trampled on. Modern China, unlike the Europe of past centuries, is in close contact with nations which have accepted a different standard of civilisation, and have small mercy for those whom, in their blindness to treasures not of steel or gold, they despise as laggards. It is not credible that the internal instability, by which China has been racked during the last quarter of a century, will for long continue. Either she will find an equilibrium for herself, and evolve a Government strong enough to maintain it; or she will be compelled, under one guise or another, to acquiesce in one imposed by foreign action.

The intention of the policy adopted at the Washington Conference was to render possible the first. It was to make a belated end of the scramble for concessions and spheres of influence which had disgraced the opening decade of the present century, and to secure China a breathing space, in which, undisturbed by foreign intervention, she could set her house in order. The aim of Japan has now been shown to be the second. It is to convert the Eastern Provinces into a Japanese protectorate; and from that vantage-ground to dominate—the historic rôle of the north—the politics of China as a whole. Whether she fails of that object, or, as at the moment seems probable, attains it, the crucial question is the future of China south of the Wall. It is there, and neither at Tokyo nor Geneva, that the fate of Manchuria will ultimately be decided. For, both culturally and in racial composition, Manchuria is Chinese to the core. Of its 30,000,000 inhabitants, 27,000,000

are Chinese; and, while Japan does not colonise, the number
of Chinese in Manchuria year by year increases.

It is true that, however the question of political sovereignty
is settled, that of the control of economic development will
remain to be decided. It will make all the difference, nevertheless, whether the conditions in which development takes place
are determined by a Chinese or an alien Government, and
that issue will depend on the course of political evolution in
China herself. If Manchuria is detached from China, it will be
because Japan commands the resources of an organised state,
while China does not. If China acquires them, it is to her, not
to Japan, that Manchuria will gravitate. As far, in short, as
Manchuria is concerned, China can afford to wait, provided
that, while waiting, she succeeds in achieving internal stability.
What are the conditions of success?

They are partly political, partly economic, partly psychological
and social. The last two have received from Chinese thinkers
more attention than the first. But, in the present circumstances
of China, the maxim *l'économique prime la politique* is less true
than its converse. Economic progress is paralysed by political
anarchy, and will continue, till order exists, to be fitful and
intermittent. The first problem, therefore, is to create an
efficient system of government.

It is a problem to be attacked piecemeal. China is too vast,
too diverse in conditions, and, in the absence of adequate communications, too amorphous and unmanageable, for it to be
possible for all parts of the country to advance together. The
process of unifying her must be carried out gradually and step
by step. There must be provinces which lead, and provinces
which follow. Some region must play the part of Prussia and
Piedmont in the Europe of the nineteenth century, serve as a
basis where reform can mobilise its forces, and spread new
standards of public spirit, efficiency and good government by
the influence of its example.

Nor, in view of the economic geography of China, can there

be serious doubt where that base is to be found. Even apart from the situation created by the Japanese invasion, Manchuria, in spite of the advanced economic life of its eastern portions, is semi-colonial. North China, which means in effect the valley of the Yellow River, including Kansu, Shensi, Shansi, and large parts, at least, of Hopei, Honan and Shantung, is economically primitive, a population of agriculturalists engaged in a desperate struggle with nature, and taking refuge, when the strain becomes intolerable, in banditry, war or migration to Manchuria, with neither the surplus resources nor the mentality required to support a modern state. The region which remains, China south of the Yellow River and east of the railway from Tientsin to Pukow, with a population of, perhaps, 250,000,000, holds the key to the future. It is watered by the greatest artery of trade in China, and one of the greatest in the world, the Yangtze River; accounts for two-thirds of the customs revenue; contains the greater part of the railway mileage outside Manchuria, some twelve out of about fifteen cities with a population of more than 200,000, nearly the whole, again excepting Manchuria, of Chinese industrialism, and the great majority of modern educational institutions. It is here, if anywhere, that a modern state can be created.

This region itself, however, the heart of modern China, is torn by violent dissensions. War between Nanking and Canton ended only in December, 1931, under the shock of the Japanese invasion; parts of the area in question are plagued with bandits, other parts with generals; there are large *enclaves*, the so-called communist areas in Kiangsi, Hunan and Fukien, in which the writ of the Government does not run. The Cantonese revolt was, doubtless, not unprovoked; but launched, as it was, on the eve of the gravest crisis in recent Chinese history, it was a tragic example of disunion. Canton, however, with its long commercial contacts with the West, and its strong provincial pride, has political traditions of its own. Even if on friendly terms with Nanking, it will owe little to its leadership. The territory effectively controlled by the National Government, where it can make its will felt decisively and at once, would be in Europe a great nation; but it consists, perhaps, of not more than half a dozen provinces, of which the most important are Kiangsu, Chekiang, Anhwei, and parts of Hopei and Shantung. Its aggregate population may be in the region of 100,000,000.

If a Government is to count anywhere, it must begin by counting at home. The impressions of a visitor are necessarily superficial; but, in view of the necessity of establishing a nucleus of good government in China, he may be pardoned for thinking that it is to the improvement of the conditions of life in these provinces that the attention of the state should first be directed. It is not a question, of course, of endorsing the view expressed by some foreigners that, in order to escape from disorder, China requires to be broken into smaller units. The result of such a policy, could it be applied, would be an eternity of civil war; but its application is impossible. Economically, as in the crucial matter of customs and railways, China, for all her diversity of conditions, is one. Politically, she is treated as one by foreign Powers. In culture and spirit, she has possessed for many centuries a unity more profound than that of some societies whose governmental machinery is more highly centralised. In no country is the impression of the nation, not merely as a territorial unit or a political system, but as a living personality, more insistent and irresistible. The sane policy is not to impair that unity, but to find means of extending it from the cultural sphere to that of political organisation. The solution of the problem must be the task of generations, but the first step towards it is to find a leverage. It is to establish a secure base, in which the state does efficiently what a state should do, and from which, when sure of itself, it can extend its influence into regions at present beyond its control.

There are obvious difficulties, economic and political, in limiting liabilities; but no other course is so likely to yield positive results in a reasonably short time. It does not seem reasonable to spend money in despatching expeditions against communists in Kiangsi or Fukien, while, as was the case two years ago, bandits are levying blackmail on villages within ten miles of Nanking, or to invite foreign experts to give advice—valuable though their help is—as to the improvement of the agricultural system, while peasants are being robbed within walking distance of the capital. The course of wisdom, it may be suggested, is, as far as is possible, not to disperse effort, but to concentrate it. It is to use authority first, where it can be used most effectively. It is to make the provinces directly under the eyes of the Government a model of order, security and efficiency; to suppress ruthlessly the exploitation of their inhabitants by tax-collectors, officials, moneylenders, landlords and bandits; and to equip them with modern roads, a modern police system, modern public health services and modern schools. It is, in short, where good administration is possible, to prove by ocular demonstration what good administration means. Such a policy is not alien, after all, to the traditions of a people which is singularly susceptible to the moral appeal of a disinterested example. In the China of the past it was not unknown for communities harassed by tyranny or disorder to request a prince of better repute to accept them as his subjects. If modern Chinese Governments relied more on the prestige which public opinion —in China an immense force—accords to positive achievements, and to them alone, they would need fewer bayonets to maintain their power.

Much, doubtless, has been done which it would be ungenerous to ignore; but much remains to do. It cannot seriously be argued that, even in the neighbourhood of Nanking, satisfactory conditions obtain. Their absence hitherto is no reflection on the Government; miracles cannot be performed in four years. Their continued absence would be a different question. It would discredit the idea of reconstruction by suggesting that it was a paper scheme not intended for application. Not only Governments, but the very idea of government, is unpopular in China. It has every reason to be; it has meant little during the last decade but taxation and war. A state cannot exist without citizens; and, if a Chinese state is to be a reality, it must win the confidence of common men. To win their confidence, it must offer practical advantages, which are clear and unmistakable. It must show results which touch directly the lives of the mass of the population. It should be least difficult to show them, where Government is not a remote abstraction, but stands close to the people. The right policy is to lay a patch of concrete where it can most easily be laid. It is to assemble in the home provinces the material and moral resources which make a modern state, and, strengthened by the prestige which only a visible example of good government can give, to advance step by step towards enlarging the area to which the same methods can be applied.

If that policy—if any policy—is to be carried out in practice, the machinery of government requires to be strengthened. Chinese thinkers not infrequently censure the present régime for its intolerance of criticism, its interference with liberty, its drastic censorship of the Press, its virtual prohibition of political meetings. They describe it as a military despotism with a civilian propaganda department. The justice of their complaints is not easily disputed; it is true that the authorities, in their reluctance to submit to the inconvenience of public criticism, deprive themselves of the advantage of public support.[1] As far, however, as the practical work of government is concerned, the gravest weakness of the system is of another kind. It consists less in its principles than in their application, or the failure to apply them. It is the absence of efficient administration, and, indeed, apart from exceptional individuals, of any adequate idea of what administration means. The main political requirement of China at the present stage of her development is the creation of an effective administrative system.

China is a country in which literary scholarship has enjoyed for many centuries exceptional prestige. The respect for it, in

[1] It is stated that the policy of the Government in these matters has undergone a change in the last nine months and that the criticisms in question are no longer so applicable as they were.

itself an admirable trait, sometimes appears to have coloured, with unfortunate results, the conceptions held of the nature of government. The belief that to write words on paper is to perform an act seems to be almost ineradicable. The result is that politics too often end where they should begin, with the assertion of intentions. In the West there are means without ends; in China ends without means. Conference follows conference, programme programme, and report report. The legislative output is enormous; the compilations of departments voluminous and instructive. Mountains of paper are accumulated; but there is no adequate machinery for transmitting power, and the wheels do not turn. It is as though, when an engine did not move, the crew, instead of repairing it, wrote a minute on the breakdown, and passed a resolution that it should start next day.

The forms of the Constitution are elaborate and unimportant. They are the product, partly of the genius of Dr. Sun Yat-sen, partly of an American version of western political theory, partly of the influence of the Russian example, partly of military exigencies. The reality, if military affairs be left on one side, is a bureaucracy. The bureaucracy is the representative institution of modern China. It is, so far as politics are concerned, the new China, the China of western education, which is engaged in a struggle with the old, the China of economic stagnation, and primitive superstitions, and bloody-minded militarists—and also, it must be added, of fastidious culture and a noble dignity of manners. In so far as the future is being determined, not by impersonal forces, or by the mere obstinate refusal to die of an older order of things, but by intelligence, knowledge, and an attempt to plan for the public good, it is by this bureaucracy and the men composing it that the future is being prepared.

In considering government in China, as in considering industry, it is necessary to remember that the prevalent conceptions of its meaning and functions are not those of the West. Except in small circles directly influenced by western ideas, and sometimes even in them, the assumptions and objectives accepted are radically different. The contrast could be illustrated in a score of different ways, but one example must suffice. Law, it is perhaps true to say, is commonly regarded less as a general rule to be universally enforced, than as the statement of an ideal to which approximation is desirable, but which must be modified in practice to meet the varying circumstances of particular cases. The principle is unimportant compared with the exigencies of the individual or group to which it must be applied. The quality which evokes admiration is less the fearless impartiality of the upright judge—that would seem crude, harsh and inhuman—than the tact of the wise and suave arbitrator who reconciles disputants by the skilful accommodation of conflicting claims.

The executive aspects of government are marked by the same studied avoidance of precise definition. The aim of military strategy in the West is to force a decision, "to seek out and destroy the main forces of the enemy." It is hardly an exaggeration to say that in China it is the opposite; it is to manœuvre so that a decision may be avoided, until the strain of forces skilfully held in suspense is resolved by circumstances. The object of the official charged with administrative duties is less to impose the law on recalcitrant wills than so to comport himself that a direct collision of wills may be avoided, even if the law suffers in the process. Hence behind political terms which China shares with the West lies a profound difference of spirit. Chinese ministers are literally ministers; they are servants, not masters. Where the West creates in its departments of state a hierarchy of authority, with the responsibilities of different grades exactly defined, a Chinese department is a group. The individual shelters himself behind it, and responsibility is diffused over its different members.

It is noticeable, indeed, how precisely the style of behaviour which appeals to Europeans arouses in Chinese uneasiness or disgust. It was the lot of the writer to be present in the capital in the spring of 1931, when the President shut the mouth of a prominent, but reputedly cantankerous, politician, by summarily imprisoning him. He discussed the step taken, the sensation of the moment, with British and Chinese acquaintances of equal experience and sagacity. The former applauded it as the decisive action of a strong man. The latter shook their heads; the person might be impossible, but the President should have held his hand till the situation found its own dénouement. In their estimate of the psychology of their countrymen they were unquestionably right. The episode raised the curtain on the Canton revolt.

To discuss in the abstract which of these different conceptions of government is to be preferred is waste of breath. Western legalism and "efficiency" have, it would probably be admitted, their ugly side. All one can say is that, if certain results are desired, certain methods must be employed. In the China of a century ago the traditional system worked; the material to be handled was not unmanageable. In the China of to-day it does not; one cannot run a railway, or administer the public finances of a modern state, or enforce a complicated code of legislation touching every side of economic life, on the basis of a system of personal understandings. But, beneath the new forms, the old tradition goes on. The bureaucracy, for all the admirable qualities of many of its individual members, is hampered by it. It is often judged unfairly by western observers, because they apply to it criteria which the public opinion of China does not yet accept.

It is exposed, in addition, to difficulties springing from the circumstances of the moment. It is necessarily, through no fault of its own, without professional traditions, for there has been no time to create them. It is harassed, again not through its own fault, by financial uncertainties, and by the insecurity of tenure inseparable from a system under which the disappearance of a minister may mean the dismissal of his staff. In spite of the existence of a body with functions analogous, on paper, to those of the British Civil Service Commission, it appears still to be appointed largely by personal influence. It is exposed to the pressure, sometimes almost irresistible, of the Chinese family system, whose claims to consideration it is a scandal to ignore. It lacks the guidance and restraint of clear rules of law, enforced by tribunals independent of the Government. Confronted with administrative problems which would baffle a specialist, it has to solve them without having had the opportunity to acquire specialised knowledge.

Nor has its previous education always done much to prepare it for its task. Whether educated abroad, or in a Chinese university, Chinese civil servants have usually learned more of the political theory than of the political practice of the West, and more of both than of the Chinese environment in which their knowledge must be applied. Nothing is more curious to a visitor than to observe that the country of which his Chinese acquaintances know least appears, in some cases, to be China herself. He is a student of politics, and finds that they understand more of the functions of the Hague Tribunal or the Supreme Court of the United States than of the manner in which Chinese cities and villages conduct their common affairs. He is interested in economic conditions, and discovers that they are better informed as to the industrial capitalism and machine farming of the West than as to the handicrafts carried on at their doors and the agriculture of peasants within sight of the city walls. To all such statements there are, of course, numerous exceptions. It would probably be agreed, however, that the output of some Chinese state departments is somewhat disproportionate to the size of the staffs employed in them, and the practical effect of their work to the labour devoted to it. They do not at present exercise the influence on the country which it is desirable that they should, and which the quality of their personnel would entitle them to wield.

Efficient administration is a modern development in the West. It is not surprising that in China, which till recently had little need of it, it should still be in an early stage of growth. In so far as the weaknesses of the system are due, not to financial stringency or to social traditions, but to technical deficiencies, their disappearance could be hastened by consulting the experience of nations which have faced similar problems. A Government must choose its objectives for itself, as a city must decide whether to build a bridge; on the question of ends no foreign admonitions can be of service to it. Few spectacles are more ludicrous than that of the European who, all unconscious of his limitations, empties on the patient politeness of his Chinese hosts the inexhaustible vials of his raw self-sufficiency. When, however, the bridge is decided on, an engineer can advise how best to build it. Once the aims of policy are determined, the expert who has handled similar problems elsewhere can give useful advice as to the steps necessary to attain them.

The West has much to learn from China of the art of living. What she can offer in return is something less important, but, on its own lower plane, useful. It is the technical skill in manipulating the machinery of life which she has acquired in the course of the last two centuries. China has made use of it to assist her in dealing with railways, flood, drought, famine and the improvement of public health. But the organisation of public administration is a matter which also has a technical side, on which western experience has some lessons to contribute. The training and recruiting of the personnel of a Civil Service; the arrangement of work within each department, and the relations of departments to each other, to the Ministry of Finance and to the political chiefs; questions of tenure and promotion; the establishment and maintenance of contacts between central and local authorities in such a way as to maintain the necessary measure of control by the former without impairing the initiative of the latter—these are elementary, but fundamental, conditions of good government on which western countries, by prolonged experiment, have worked out a technique. There is no reason why China should proceed by the method of trial and error, or buy her experience at the cost of several decades of waste and misery.

When one turns from these general issues to those special to particular branches of administration, the need of ascertaining what is done elsewhere is even more evident. No one, however intelligent, can know by the light of nature how to promote agricultural co-operation, to improve systems of land tenure, to develop rural industries, to introduce a general system of primary education, to establish an efficient school inspectorate, to enforce factory legislation, to organise an efficient police system, or to cope with any other of the scores of administrative duties which devolve on the officials of a modern state. But these are all matters where a large body of expert knowledge is available in different countries. The sensible course for a Government which is faced with the necessity of coping for the first time with similar tasks is to ascertain the manner in which they have been undertaken elsewhere. It is not a question, of course, of aping foreign methods, but of sifting experience and consulting those who can interpret it. Chinese administration must be Chinese, not western. But, in order to be Chinese, it need not begin by repeating the errors made, and painfully overcome, by western countries. Yet it is precisely that which, through mere ignorance of their nature, it is in danger of doing.

It may be suggested, therefore, that one simple way of improving the processes of government in China would be to secure the best advice available both on the organisation of the public services in general and on the administrative technique of particular among them. What is required for the purpose is neither brief visits to China by western notabilities, nor western travel by Chinese with a view to the acquisition of general ideas, with which China is seriously over-populated already. It is, first, that the services of western officials experienced in different branches of administration should be placed at the disposal of the Chinese Government, with a view to their advising as to the organisation of particular services; and, secondly, that carefully selected Chinese civil servants should be sent to study specific departments of administration in western countries for a period sufficiently long to become thoroughly conversant with them. The League of Nations is the natural institution to assist the Chinese Government in carrying out such a policy.

For the disorders of China the West is largely responsible. Her recovery from them is one of the major interests of the world. The steps which a British Government could take to promote it have been discussed by Mr. Curtis in his valuable book.[1] But the League can do what can be done by no single state. It has already aided China by providing experts to initiate the organisation of public health, famine relief and a factory inspectorate. There is a wide range of subjects with regard to which similar action could usefully be taken. Nor should the necessity be overlooked of dealing with the more general question of the principles on which the public services are to be staffed and conducted. New branches of administration may be started with foreign advice, but they must be carried on by Chinese. It is essential to their efficiency that the personnel responsible for them should be recruited in the manner most likely to secure the best ability available, and should be organised in a way to give ability due scope.

The National Economic Council, recently established at Nanking, is an example of fruitful collaboration between the Chinese Government and advisers supplied by the League. It is important, not only because of the intrinsic importance of the subjects with which it will deal, but because its secretariat, as it gets into its stride, will set new standards of administration, and serve as the nucleus round which a well-organised Civil Service can in time be built up. Nor is it only the machinery of central government which requires to be strengthened. The improvement of local government, including the work of the agents of the central government in different localities, is at least equally important. Local government is the sphere in which the state impinges most directly on the lives of the mass of the population. If it is reasonably honest and competent, it does more for the progress of the country than a hundred programmes adopted with acclamation by a thousand conferences. If it is corrupt or inefficient, the most admirable schemes of reconstruction prepared in the capital are little more than waste paper.

Local government in China is still largely an unexplored

[1] Lionel Curtis, *The Capital Question of China*, 1932.

field. None of the score or more of professors of political
science in the fifty odd universities of the country appear to
have thought it worth while to write an account of the manner
in which more than two or three of the thirty provinces, one
hundred or so large cities, nineteen hundred *Hsien* and half a
million villages are in practice governed. As far as the provinces and more important towns are concerned, information
can, of course, be obtained. The quality of their administration
appears in some cases to be good, in others the reverse. About
the proceedings of the *Hsien* and villages, little seems to be
known. How exactly, for instance—to take one simple example,
which affects both the state and millions of individuals—
taxation on land is assessed and collected, appears, at any rate
as far as some parts of the country are concerned, to be an
almost impenetrable mystery, on which few Chinese themselves venture to speak with confidence. It is alleged, whether
with justice or not it is impossible to say, that the influence of
well-to-do proprietors causes some land, which should pay
taxation, to be under-assessed, or to escape it altogether, while
other land pays too much, and that part of the revenue sticks
to the fingers of the collectors. Apart from that particular
matter, oppression by tyrannical magistrates and the abuse of
their power by the local gentry are, if rumour may be trusted,
in certain regions common. Any general statement is at present
impossible. What appears to have occurred, however, is that
the reconstruction of government during the last twenty years
has been largely confined to the upper storeys of the system,
and that in the lower the old régime, with its old abuses, and
possibly some new ones, has continued unaltered.

Here again, if certain evils are inevitable, others certainly
are not. Here again, till the worst are removed, it is idle to
advance policies involving a large increase in the activities of
governmental bodies. And, here again, there is a large volume
of experience, both in the East and the West, from which
suggestion can be drawn. Before action can be taken, the first
necessity is to know the facts. What is needed, in the first place,
is a detailed investigation of the organisation and working of

local administration in certain areas, including villages, *Hsien* and towns, such as, failing action by the Government, could be undertaken by the Political Science and Economics Departments of a group of universities. Inquiry would reveal certain weaknesses; and the next step would be to ascertain how similar weaknesses had been corrected elsewhere. The knowledge obtained would supply a basis for reform which is at present absent. Most proposals for ameliorating the conditions of life in China, such as those concerned, for example, with the extension of education, with public health and with agriculture, would involve, if carried out, increased activity on the part either of local bodies or of local officials of the Central Government. The condition of their successful application is a corresponding, and, if possible, a preliminary, advance in methods of local administration.

An improvement in the administrative system would not necessarily involve additional expense; on the contrary, by checking waste, it would probably diminish the cost of government. If, however, it increased it, it would more than pay for itself. For it would create the stability which is the first condition of economic progress, and would make possible the application of schemes of development which are at present impracticable. The fundamental economic needs of China have been stated in the preceding pages, and need not again be discussed. They are, in the order of their importance, (i) an improvement in the means of communication, by the extension of roads, and, as circumstances allow, of railways; (ii) the improvement of agriculture, on the side, not only of productive methods, but of finance, marketing and land tenure; (iii) the development, with adequate safeguards, of machine industry, and its extension beyond the small number of areas in which at present it is concentrated. Neither political stability nor economic progress, however, will be achieved automatically. Their possibility depends on a change in the mentality of the Chinese people. What is the present position of education in China, and what part can it play in shaping her future?[1]

Apart from university education, for which the facts are known, Chinese educational statistics are not free from ambiguity; but the general features of the present situation can be briefly summarised. There were stated to exist in 1930–31, 207,520 primary schools, with 8,785,879 pupils, to which must be added a large number of undertakings of a less formal type, half schools, half a system of private tutorships, for which no figures were available. The number of secondary schools in the same year was put at 13,596, and their pupils at 783,140. The universities numbered in 1930–31 59, attended by 33,847 students; of which 15, with 11,572 students, were national, 17, with 5,910 students, provincial, and 27, with 16,365 students, private universities, registered with, and recognised by, the Ministry of Education. In addition there were 29 higher technical institutions, the majority maintained by provinces and cities; an unknown number of private institutions describing themselves as universities, but unrecognised by the state; and a considerable body of activities described by the words social education or adult education. The training of teachers is carried on partly in the senior secondary schools, partly in normal colleges; but a considerable number of teachers in primary schools have received only a primary school education. The general administrative scheme, which is subject, however, to exceptions, is that primary schools are maintained by the districts or *Hsien*, secondary schools and provincial universities by the Provinces, and national universities, together with certain cultural institutions, by the National Government. The total educational expenditure for the year 1930–31 was approximately $110,000,000 (Mex.), of which just under $15,000,000 was contributed by the National Government, just over $44,000,000 by the Provinces, and $50,500,000 by the *Hsien*.

---

[1] The Chinese educational system has recently been the subject of a Report by a Mission representing the League of Nations. I have thought it unnecessary, therefore, to do more than refer to some of its salient features.

Public education in China is the creation of the period since 1900, and, in large measure, since 1920. To have built it up in less than a generation, in the midst of civil disorder, international complications, grave financial stresses, and the recurrent calamities of flood and drought, is an extraordinary achievement. What is surprising is, not its defects, but its existence. The problem in China is not, as it was until recently in some western nations, to commend education to a country sceptical of its value. It is to base education on the real needs of China herself, not on foreign examples; to humanise it, by relating it to the practical facts of Chinese life; to stiffen standards of efficiency, both in teaching and administration; and to organise efforts at present often uncoordinated, and sometimes conflicting, into a well-balanced system.

The present weaknesses of Chinese education are, however, serious. Primary education, which should be the foundation on which the superstructure rests, is gravely deficient both in quantity and quality. What proportion of children between six and twelve years of age attend school for some period, it is impossible to say. At the outside, however, it can hardly exceed one in five, a figure rising, in certain exceptional cities and provinces, to between 30 and 40 per cent, and falling almost to zero in the more backward regions. Of those children, moreover, who do attend school, large numbers attend it for so short a time that little serious influence can be exercised by it. Secondary education nominally covers two periods of three years each, the junior secondary school extending from twelve to fifteen, and the senior secondary school from fifteen to eighteen; but the proportion who complete the whole course appears in most areas to be small. The work both of the primary and the secondary schools seems to an observer to be often—of course there are exceptions—formal, bookish and academic to a degree almost inhuman. It gives too little thought to the physical needs of the children, and makes excessive demands on their powers of attention. It overloads their memory, instead of exciting their interest and curiosity. It keeps them poring over text-books, or listening to a teacher, when they should be using their eyes and ears for purposes more important and more amusing. It makes an excessive use of oral instruction, to the neglect of practical activities and experimental work. Except here and there, it does little to prepare them to understand the life of the society to which they belong. Not infrequently, indeed, it appears expressly designed to make the rising generation stupid, nervous and unhappy, by means of education.

Universities, again with exceptions, appear to suffer from much the same defects. Owing to the weaknesses of the secondary school system, a considerable number of the students who enter them are unprepared to profit by a university education. They are over-lectured and over-examined. They read too little, do little independent work, and have few opportunities of personal contact with their teachers, who themselves lecture for an excessive number of hours per week, and too often, owing to the insecurity of their position, find it advantageous to work simultaneously for more than one institution. The curriculum is based to an excessive extent upon foreign materials. At worst, professors appear to repeat in China the substance of lectures heard, or books read, abroad. At best, insufficient attention is paid to the truism that the object of a university is not to cram students with information, but to prepare them for life in a society, and that, if a university is to aid its members to play a useful part in the life of China, it is less important that they should be informed as to the parliaments and stock exchanges of western nations, than that they should understand the political and economic conditions of their own. The result is that the whole system has the air of a thing exotic and artificial. It is top-heavy, over-intellectualised and, in some cases, pretentious. Its atmosphere is that of a hot-house, not of the open air.

Modern education in China was as inevitably based on western models as was that of Tudor England on classical antiquity. In China, as in Europe, the Renaissance had its source in the discovery of a culture formerly ignored or despised. To a generation born into a world visibly falling to pieces, the new knowledge seemed to whisper the magic word that would rebuild it. The key to a golden future, to individual success and national regeneration, could be sought at the cost of three weeks in a steamer, and, when found, could be brought home. It was natural that the vogue of western science should be immense, and its worship indiscriminate. It was not less natural that the relations of cause and effect in western history should be reversed, and that it should be supposed that western science was the parent of western civilisation, not western civilisation of western science. Thus, by an easily intelligible paradox, Chinese political nationalism found its ally and ideal in a denationalised education.

That phase—the phase of the discovery of the New Learning —produced the educational system existing to-day. It has not yet ended, but it has done its work. It created a ferment; it could do no more. The task of the next phase is more difficult, but the penalty of postponing it will be national disintegration. If education is to be alive, it must have its roots in the soil. Salvation could not be imported from the West, even if the West possessed it; it is not an article of commerce. It must come from China herself, if it is to come at all. The time has arrived when Chinese educationalists and teachers should cease scanning the horizon and observe the ground beneath their feet. It is there, or nowhere, in the practical realities of Chinese life, that they will find the only possible materials for an educational system adapted to Chinese needs.

A feature of Chinese society which surprises an observer is the division between the intelligentsia and the remainder of the population. China is not cursed to the same extent as the West with a class system based on property. Under the old régime, not wealth, but official status, raised the individual from the mass; and, since admission to an official career depended on success in examination, the prestige of the scholar was naturally immense. In the China of to-day that prestige still continues, and is even heightened, perhaps, by the respect accorded to the mastery of western science. The students form almost a separate estate. By obtaining admission to a secondary school, and still more, to a university, they become members of a small privileged class, which has rights with few duties. They appear sometimes to know little of the life of the great mass of their fellow-countrymen, and, of course with exceptions, to contribute little to its improvement. Education enables individuals to climb from one plane to another; but it has hitherto done little to raise the general level of intellectual attainment and social well-being. Till the gulf has been spanned, national unity is a phrase. The natural agency to supply the piers of the bridge is primary education. What is required is both an improvement in its quality and a large increase in the number of children brought within its scope.

Given a realistic attitude in teachers and administrators, the first change could be effected in a reasonably short time. It is a question, not of new machinery, but of a change of spirit. There is no reason why, instead of being the rather dreary book-worm factories, which, with the best intentions, some of them are to-day, primary schools should not do far more than they do to meet certain simple and fundamental human needs. They could train children, for example, in the care of the body and in a healthy regimen of life. They could offer them opportunities of practical work—simple carpentry, gardening, the care of plants and animals. They could prepare them to understand their immediate environment by burning nine-tenths of the books in use, and making agriculture, village handicrafts, and the local system of communications the basis of lessons in geography, history and the study of nature. They could abolish, in short, the dreadful régime of talk and text-books imported from the West, which the West —alas, how slowly!—is now discarding. The truism that the business of a school is not to prepare children to fit into the moulds, or acquire the formulae, thought desirable by adults, but to enable them, when they are children, to be healthy, and, if possible, happy, children, must in China, as elsewhere, be the foundation of reform.

The problem of securing a wider extension of primary education is more difficult; but, in the opinion of good judges, it is not insoluble. In the most advanced provinces and cities, for example, Chekiang, Kiangsu, Hangchow and Tientsin, the percentage of children already attending, for a longer or shorter period, the primary schools, is not less than it was in the England of 1850. In such areas it would be possible, provided due notice were given of the change, to introduce a system of compulsory school attendance. The reasonable course would appear to be for the Ministry of Education to schedule certain of them, where the circumstances are most favourable to educational development, as regions to which the measure is to be applied at a date in the future fixed by it; to undertake, in co-operation with the local administrative authorities, a survey of their resources in the shape of accommodation and teachers; and to begin at once to make, with their assistance, the necessary preparations. The important point is not that the policy should, in the first place, be widely applied, but that it should be brought into operation in those parts of the country where, owing to the progress already made, there is a reasonable prospect of its being successful.

Secondary education, like primary, suffers from an intolerable bookishness. The schools are too uniform in type; there are few with a curriculum which is realistic in the sense that it employs as its material the work of agriculture and industry, and groups other subjects round them. Though in theory the senior secondary school provides vocational courses, in addition to a general cultural course preparing students for the university and to the training of teachers, in practice such courses appear frequently to be absent. The result is that pupils who have little aptitude for letters pursue, under the name of general education, what is in reality a specialised literary course, and that China is offered by her schools an excessive supply of journalists and rhetoricians, when what she most requires is trained practical intelligence. Here again, what is most needed is nothing subtle or recondite, but merely to act on the truism that children do not cease to be children because they happen to be described as students. The curriculum requires to be simplified and lightened; the hours of instruction substantially reduced; the leisure for recreation and open-air activities greatly enlarged; the opportunities for independent work by the pupils, individually and in groups, greatly extended. Existing senior secondary schools should be required, as a condition of continued recognition by the Ministry, to provide practical and vocational courses. The establishment of new schools, giving only a general cultural education, should not in future be sanctioned, except on proof being given to the Ministry that they are genuinely required.

An improvement in the quality of secondary education would raise the standard of work done in the universities. The progress made by university education in China has been astonishing. It has been created almost from nothing in the course of little more than a quarter of a century, and no admiration can be too great for the energy thrown into developing it. The very rapidity of its expansion, however, has created problems which are still unsolved. Certain universities are institutions of which any nation might be proud. Certain others suffer from grave, but remediable, defects, which, in view of the great influence exercised by universities in China, it is important to remove.

The weaknesses of the system are a matter partly of organisation, partly of educational methods. On the one hand, the geographical distribution of the universities is at present somewhat capricious; twenty-five out of the fifty-nine, and 60 per cent of all the university students in China, were found in 1930 in, or in the immediate neighbourhood of, two cities, Peiping and Shanghai. The multiplicity of separate universities in the same area means too often that there are several weak institutions, instead of one or two strong ones, and causes much needless duplication of work. The insecurity of the finances of the national universities, arising from the fact that funds due from the Government are often in arrears, causes the position of their staffs to be highly precarious, and results in the disastrous practice of teachers, in order to supplement their incomes, taking work at more than one institution.

On the other hand, some proportion of the students admitted

to universities are not qualified to pursue university studies, with the result that they profit little themselves, and drag down the standard of the institutions concerned. The reliance on lectures, copied from the lips of professors and memorised for the purpose of the four annual examinations, is carried to such lengths that students may actually spend twenty-five hours or more a week in listening to them, and is fatal to serious work on the part both of the students and, sometimes, of their teachers. As in other educational institutions, the use made of foreign materials is not infrequently excessive, with the result that observation and reflection are sacrificed to the acquisition of information, some of which is almost meaningless to its recipients, because it has little relevance to the facts of their own experience and environment. Owing partly to the time devoted to the oral exposition of the rudiments of subjects to large bodies of students, partly to the prevalence of the practice of pluralism among teachers, which arises from the uncertainty of their financial position, there is little intimate contact between students and staffs outside the lecture-room. As a consequence the life of certain universities appears to be distracted by a chronic condition of exasperation, resulting in periodical revolts by the students against the university authorities, which paralyses their educational activities and creates the worst conceivable atmosphere for young men to grow up in.

As in other countries, the professions and the public services in China are largely recruited from the universities. The effects of such phenomena on the public life of the country are, therefore, serious. It is utopian to expect an intelligent policy of reconstruction to be planned and carried out by men who, as students, have learned little of the realities of Chinese life, and have been accustomed to defy any regulation which they regard as inconvenient. Scholars of high distinction have studied and taught in Chinese universities, and great services have been rendered by her universities to China. It is significant, however, that Chinese themselves frequently express the opinion that the universities have deteriorated, both in intellectual standards and in *moral*, in the last ten years.

Whether that view is justified or not, a visitor cannot say. It is not open to question that certain, at any rate, of the weaknesses which give rise to criticism could be removed, provided that the authorities of the leading universities and the Ministry of Education would agree on a policy and pursue it steadily over a period of years. On the side of organisation, the first need is that the financial position of the universities should be stabilised, and that grants once promised should be punctually paid. At the same time it appears reasonable that the Government, since it provides nine-tenths of the income of the national universities, should require that needless overlapping, with all the waste which it involves, shall be avoided, and that, when several universities exist in a single area, they shall be combined, so far, at any rate, as to form constituent parts of a federal university. Were these two reforms, both repeatedly urged by Chinese educationalists, adopted, it would be possible to ensure that university staffs were paid with regularity, and that in return they devoted their whole time to a single institution. If, in addition, universities in different parts of the country would establish, either by voluntary agreement or under pressure from the Ministry, a common entrance examination of a reasonably exacting character, the deterioration of intellectual standards which takes place to-day could largely be checked.

Questions of organisation, though important, are not the central problem. The root of the matter was expressed, perhaps, by the Chinese president of a university, when he complained that the universities were on the way to be commercialised. The economic pressure on students to obtain degrees, and on teachers to see that they are obtained, is severe. With certain exceptions, universities have succumbed to it. As a result, it is hardly an exaggeration to say that in some of them everyone graduates and no one is educated. What a country requires, however, is men with education, not graduates without it. If the universities are to serve the needs of China, the weaker among them must change their view of their function, and submit to a somewhat drastic revision of their methods. Quality must cease to be sacrificed to the clamour for mass production, even though the result is a temporary diminution in the number of students. Emphasis must be laid, not on supplying them with the information required to enable them to pass examinations, but—a more exacting task—on teaching them to think.

Reform will not be easy. Students, would-be students, and the relatives of both, are a powerful vested interest. A university education opens doors to careers that would otherwise be closed. Not only is it, as in other countries, an investment, but, owing to the backwardness of economic development in China, it is almost the only investment by which escape can be achieved into a life of comparative dignity and ease. Reform, however, is essential. Unless the nation is supplied by its educational system with a larger number of men who have undergone the discipline of serious intellectual work, and— equally important—have learned to apply their training to the special problems of China, she will neither improve the conditions of her economic life nor achieve internal stability.

The particular measures most urgently needed are, perhaps, six. First, as stated above, the standard of attainment required as a condition of admission to a university should be raised. Second, the part played by lecturing should be substantially reduced, and part of the time gained should be used for the purpose of personal tuition, seminar and laboratory work. Third, the system under which students graduate piecemeal by means of a series of "credits," acquired at intervals during the whole course of their university life, in subjects taken one by one, and dropped when the necessary percentage of marks in the four annual examinations has been obtained, should be abandoned, and two examinations, one held in the middle, and one at the end, of the university course, should be substituted for it. Fourth, a larger space in the curriculum should be given to studies directly concerned with the life of China, and teachers should not be appointed, at any rate to the departments concerned with the social sciences, unless they have shown that they are competent to handle Chinese materials. Fifth, teachers must understand that a university is not merely a collection of lecture-rooms, but a spiritual society, and that their function is to establish personal relations with students sufficiently cordial to enable them to be accepted as consultants and advisers. Sixth, a Universities Council, composed of representatives of the universities and of persons nominated by the Ministry of Education, should be established, to advise the latter as to the institutions to be recognised, to administer grants, to lay down the conditions with which, as a condition of receiving them, universities must comply, and to exercise a general supervision over the interests and progress of university education. The phase of expansion has done its work. What is needed now is consolidation.

In all periods of reconstruction the eye may rest either on the creative forces which are building a new world, or on the débris of the old which encumber the ground, and amid which the masons must stumble to their task. It is tempting to seize, as the special characteristic of China, on the stamp set on her social organisation by the legacy of the past. Since the past is the only material which is given to mankind for the fashioning of the future, that feature of her life is properly emphasised. If, however, on the first view, the note of China seems, not change, but permanence, on maturer reflection change seems no less significant than features which are unchanging. The problem—a problem not only for the student, but still more for the statesman—is to do equal justice to both the old and the new. The balance is not easily maintained, and there are precipices on either hand.

Much talk of the Westernisation of China is remote from realities. It is a kind of incantation, which proceeds, not only from foreigners, but, occasionally, also from Chinese themselves. The contrast between Chinese and western civilisation heightens the impression which the latter makes on them, so that the formula derives part of its magic from the very circumstances which make it incapable of application. Young

men educated abroad are swept off their feet by their first
glimpse of the comfort and power of a new world. Conscious
of the feebleness of their country, and eager for its progress,
they would lift its burden by transplanting to it the apparatus
of material prosperity whose vast power has dazzled them.
China requires, it is true, the scientific and technological
equipment of the West; poverty and weakness such as she
endures to-day are dreadful evils. If western nations could
bring themselves, instead of regarding her as a field of enterprise, to realise that, on a long view, her major interests are
also theirs, and to help her to attain them, they would reap
a harvest of gratitude which would more than repay them.
But the problem is more complicated: *porro unum necessarium*.
The machinery is useless or destructive in the absence of a
philosophy of life to control and direct it. The West staggers
blindly for lack of one, helpless amid powers it is unable to
use. It cannot give to the East what it does not possess. Itself
bewildered and confused, it can bring to China, in the realm
of ideas, little but uncertainty and confusion.

Thus the imitation of America or Europe, which has profoundly influenced Chinese education, offers no solution of
the deeper problems of China. It was a necessary stage in
her evolution; till she knew the West, she could not fully
know herself. For certain of her difficulties, foreign experience
still has useful lessons to teach. Critically sifted, by minds which
know what to reject as well as what to accept, it can offer
suggestions as to economic organisation, social policy and
administration which may aid China in equipping herself
with the structural framework of an ordered state. But, though
a nation may borrow its tools from abroad, for the energy to
handle them it must look within.

> Erquickung hast du nicht gewonnen,
> Wenn sie dir nicht aus eigner Seele quillt.

It is in herself alone, in her own historical culture, redis-
covered and reinterpreted in the light of her modern require-

ments, that China will find the dynamic which she needs. The most fundamental achievements of her revolution are still to come. The problem is to translate political rejuvenation into the practical terms of social institutions, and to build with a modern technique, but on Chinese foundations. It is to her schools and universities that she must look for the builders.

TABLE I*

INDICES OF INDUSTRIAL DEVELOPMENT IN CHINA

	1896	1900	1910	1913	1920	1925	1926	1927	1928	1929	1930
Cotton Mills (thousands)	12	17	26	28	54	118	118	119	120	—	127
Cotton Spindles (thousands)	417	565	831	1,210	1,650	3,569	3,414	3,612	3,613	—	4,223
Cotton Looms (hundreds)	21	—	—	—	95	216	259	298	298	—	293
Flour Mills	—	3	31	57	141	176	—	—	193	193	—
Factories in Shanghai (over thirty workers)†	—	—	—	70	192	316	381	449	540	648	—
Factories in Tientsin†	—	—	—	34	135	358	—	—	—	—	—
Factories in China (over thirty workers; not including Tientsin)	—	—	—	—	—	—	—	—	—	785	837
Iron Ore production (thousand tons approx.)	—	—	—	245	673	1,099	1,223	1,347	1,542	1,747	1,975
Pig Iron production (thousand tons approx.)	—	—	—	959	1,865	1,519	1,561	1,710	2,003	—	—
Coal Production (million tons)	—	—	—	14·0	21·3	24·3	21·5	23·0	24·2	25·1	—
Motor Vehicles in China (approx. number, thousands)	—	—	—	—	2·6	8·8	12·8	13·2	30·0	35·0	35
Imports of Gasoline (million gallons)	—	—	—	150	258	200	300	411	433	—	—
Miles of Motor Roads (approx., thousands)	—	—	0·2	0·5	0·6	14·0	15·5	16·5	18·5	34·8	—
Miles of Railways (approx.)	250	1,500	4,500	5,400	6,500	7,500	—	8,750	—	9,500	—
Exports (quantity index)	—	—	—	100·0	119·4	140·9	149·6	163·4	165·5	—	—
Imports (quantity index)	—	—	—	100·0	106·5	157·0	186·7	157·2	188·3	—	—
Steamers entered and cleared (tons)	—	—	—	87,614	99,642	124,516	132,249	112,048	148,261	150,203	—
Imports of Raw Cotton (thousand piculs)	—	135	206	134	678	1,607	2,745	2,415	1,916	2,515	—
Exports of Cotton Shirting (thousand pieces)	—	—	—	—	58	1,289	1,536	2,593	2,143	2,249	—
Exports of all Cotton Piece Goods (thousand pieces)	—	—	—	579	858	1,805	1,922	3,085	2,749	—	—
Exports of Silk Piece Goods (hundred pieces, including pongees)	208	183	300	345	375	313	387	328	331	296	—
Exports of Bean Cake (million piculs)	—	1·8	7·4	11·8	19·0	20·7	26·1	24·3	21·4	18·7	—
Exports of Bean Oil (thousand piculs)	—	280	571	492	1,713	1,989	2,667	2,469	942	1,115	—
Imports of Machinery (million Hk. Taels)	—	1·5	1·0	4·6	22·3	—	—	18·8	20·3	29·9	—

* I am indebted to Mr. W. Holland for help in compiling this table.
† Includes only carpet weaving, hosiery knitting, cotton and rayon weaving establishments.

TABLE II

This and the following Tables are based on the results of an investigation carried out by the Ministry of Industries between April and September, 1930 (*General Statistics of Factories in China, 1930*). For a discussion of the figures, see above, pp. 124–127.

STATISTICS OF INDUSTRY BY PROVINCES IN 1930

Province	Number of Factories	Capital*	Number of Workers†	Power	Annual Value‡ of Product
		Dollars*			Dollars*
Kiangsu ..	1,116	250,851,542	279,056	152,191 H.P. 545,052 K.W. 3,290 K.V.A.	214,129,021
Chekiang ..	62	10,743,005	23,233	3,483 H.P. 28,233 K.W.	24,205,868
Anhwei ..	17	3,183,200	3,786	5,750 H.P.	4,413,900
Kiangsi ..	12	3,097,800	3,460	2,322 HP.	2,808,840
Hupeh ..	108	26,584,183	51,054	46,990 HP. 1,285 K.W. 314 Am.	52,027,927
Shantung (Tsingtao only) ..	44	26,095,500	19,861	10,616 H.P.	6,528,320
Mukden ..	351	44,469,722	898,467§	6,581 H.P. 1,000 K.W.	33,026,666
Kirin ..	113	18,261,000	8,340	8,523 H.P.	8,396,920
Heilungkiang	20	4,545,000	1,038	1,944 H.P.	13,358,850
Hopei (Shun-teh only) ..	31	582,300	9,645	1,365 H.P.	13,222,400
Kwangtung..	75	7,191,950	9,638	197,210 H.P.	7,170,303
Fukien ..	22	4,632,250	2,399	1,774 H.P. 2,675 K.W.	3,630,000
Kwangsi ..	4	309,000	249	206 H.P.	459,000

* *I.e.*, paid-up capital. All values in the table are stated in Chinese silver dollars.
† These figures are not in all cases complete.
‡ Value of product = total factory costs.
§ This figure is obviously an error. It appears to arise from assigning, presumably through a misprint, 605,404 textile workers to Liaoyang.

TABLE III

NUMBER OF FACTORY WORKERS AND VALUE OF PRODUCT IN DIFFERENT
INDUSTRIES IN TWENTY-NINE CITIES IN 1930

	Number of Workers	Per Cent	Annual Value* of Product (in Dollars*)	Per Cent
Textiles†	566,301	47·2	279,598,918	46·6
Preparation of Food and Tobacco	176,504	14·7	102,768,509	17·1
Clothing	80,078	6·6	3,042,771	0·5
Building	77,737	6·5	33,414,067	5·6
Chemicals	72,020	5·9	97,281,079	16·2
Machinery	65,501	5·4	15,414,291	2·6
Educational Supplies ..	59,006	4·9	6,578,914	1·1
Furniture	40,195	3·3	1,413,654	0·2
Art Products	10,216	0·8	50,000	—
Public Utilities	5,432	0·4	21,843,961	3·6
Construction of Vehicles	1,284	0·1	34,444,608	5·8
Unclassified	50,044	4·2	4,007,700	0·7
Total	1,204,318		599,858,472	

* See notes to previous Table.
† The principal branches of the textile industry were cotton spinning (206,532 workers), silk reeling (148,814 workers), cotton weaving (109,809 workers), hosiery knitting (21,452 workers), silk weaving (26,448 workers).

TABLE IV

NUMBER OF FACTORIES WITH THIRTY OR MORE WORKERS IN CHINA
(EXCLUDING TIENTSIN)

Town	1911	1920	1925	1930
Shanghai	48	192	406	837
Wusih	8	43	59	153
Dairen	39	118	146	152
Hankow	15	38	54	76
Canton	3	17	28	63
Harbin	5	26	40	57
Hangchow	4	19	28	50
Tsingtao	—	12	21	44
Antung	1	20	32	39
Nanking	1	3	12	28
Nantung	5	10	13	15
All China (excluding Tientsin)	171	673	1,099	1,975

TABLE V

DISTRIBUTION OF FACTORIES WITH THIRTY OR MORE WORKERS IN TOWNS
(EXCLUDING TIENTSIN)

Number of Factories	Number of Towns		
	1911	1920	1930
1 to 5	30	44	51
6 ,, 10	5	23	35
11 ,, 15	3	15	25
16 ,, 20	2	9	19
21 ,, 25	2	5	16
26 ,, 50	2	5	16
51 ,, 75	—	2	6
76 ,, 100	—	2	4
101 ,, 150	—	2	3
151 ,, 500	—	1	3
500 or more	—	—	1

This Table, which is also based on the results of the investigation carried out by
(Vol. IV, No. 38, September 21, 1931). Though not completely accurate, it gives
The industries covered by it are textiles, chemicals, the preparation of food and
the construction of vehicles, public utilities, and building. Only establishments
include the value of food, if any, supplied by employers. The dollars, as elsewhere,

EARNINGS AND HOURS OF INDUSTRIAL WORKERS

City			Total Number of Workers	Average Earnings		
				Men		
				Max.	Min.	Mode
				Dollars	Dollars	Dollars
Shanghai	..	..	362,894	50.00	8.00	15.28
Wusih	..	..	70,688	30.00	7.77	20.00
Nantung	..	..	12,627	35.00	6.00	23.11
Soochow	..	..	58,814	35.00	7.00	16.00
Wuching	..	..	16,219	34.00	5.50	14.00
Ihing	..	..	12,570	43.00	7.00	13.50
Kiangtu (Yangchow)	..		1,669	23.00	4.00	8.10
Chingkiang	..	..	9,033	42.30	6.00	15.00
Nanking	..	..	17,887	30.00	6.50	10.80
Hangchow	..	..	16,171	38.00	7.20	13.50
Ningpo	..	..	4,477	24.00	7.50	24.00
Chiahsing	..	..	7,080	40.00	4.00	22.20
P'engpu	..	..	7,678	30.00	8.00	10.80
Wuhu	..	..	15,835	35.60	4.00	16.00
Anch'ing	..	..	5,243	26.00	3.00	8.40
Kiukiang	..	..	2,113	29.66	6.00	15.00
Nanchang	..	..	6,882	22.88	5.50	13.00
Hankow	..	..	169,892	41.00	8.00	19.50
Wuchang	..	..	23,974	30.25	9.00	18.00
Tayeh	..	..	3,936	—	—	16.00
Tsingtao	..	..	26,428	24.00	8.00	15.00
Canton	..	..	239,365	30.00	7.50	10.62
Wuchow	..	..	2,331	29.16	4.56	22.50
Ch'aoan	..	..	10,538	—	—	27.50
Fushan	..	..	17,855	48.12	6.67	12.50
Swatow	..	..	6,871	35.00	7.66	15.54
Shunteh	..	..	54,449	18.83	5.00	18.83
Amoy	..	..	4,767	40.00	18.00	24.00
Foochow	..	..	16,032	33.00	12.00	18.00

VI

the Ministry of Industries, is reproduced from the *Nankai Weekly Statistical Service*
the latest information available as to monthly earnings and as to hours in 29 cities.
tobacco, clothing, furniture making, machinery, educational supplies, art products,
employing thirty or more workers are included. The figures of earnings do not
are Mexican dollars.

IN TWENTY-NINE CITIES OF CHINA IN 1930

| per Person per Month | | | | | | Average Working Hours per Day | | |
| Women | | | Children | | | | | |
Max.	Min.	Mode	Max.	Min.	Mode	Max.	Min.	Mode
Dollars	Dollars	Dollars	Dollars	Dollars	Dollars			
24.00	7.00	12.50	21.00	5.00	8.07	12	8	11
21.00	15.00	17.10	13.50	9.00	10.50	12	7	10
13.47	5.00	13.47	9.75	4.39	8.59	12	6	8
25.00	9.00	15.00	16.00	3.00	9.00	14	7	10
13.97	7.50	11.50	9.45	4.75	6.75	12	7	10
—	—	12.00	17.10	2.00	9.60	10	6	6
—	—	8.10	—	—	2.00	13	8	10
15.00	7.20	15.00	10.50	2.00	10.50	12	7	9
—	—	—	—	—	7.50	12	6	10
20.40	8.00	12.33	—	—	5.10	12	7	11
18.00	8.00	9.00	—	—	6.00	10	8	8
22.00	9.00	19.87	15.60	6.00	15.60	12	8	10
24.00	8.90	8.90	—	—	9.00	11	8	9
—	—	12.60	—	—	7.20	14	8	12
—	—	6.50	—	—	6.00	12	8	10
—	—	15.00	—	—	6.50	10	7	9
—	—	—	—	—	—	14	8	14
19.20	6.00	19.20	9.00	3.00	4.50	14	8	10
17.00	—	12.93	9.00	—	8.46	12	9	12
—	—	—	—	—	6.00	—	—	8
—	—	15.00	—	—	10.00	12	8	12
—	—	7.50	—	—	6.00	14	8	9
—	—	10.50	—	—	4.00	12	7	9
—	—	—	—	—	—	12	9	12
—	—	6.00	—	—	3.75	14	8	10
22.00	—	8.00	13.00	2.00	6.00	12	8	8
—	—	18.75	—	—	8.40	15	9	10
20.00	10.50	20.00	10.00	—	8.00	15	8	8
21.00	10.00	12.00	9.00	3.00	8.00	10	6	10

INDEX